Big-leaf Rhododendrons
Growing the giants of the genus

Publication of this book was made possible through the generous assistance and support of the Pukeiti Rhododendron Trust and the TSB Community Trust.

Text © Glyn Church & Graham Smith, 2015
Typographical design © David Bateman Ltd, 2015
Photographs © Pat Greenfield, 2015 (unless credited otherwise)

Published in 2015 by David Bateman Ltd
30 Tarndale Grove, Albany, Auckland, New Zealand

www.batemanpublishing.co.nz

ISBN 978-1-86953-912-2

This book is copyright. Except for the purpose of fair review, no part may be stored or transmitted in any form or by any means, electronic or mechanical, including recording or storage in any information retrieval systems, without permission in writing from the publisher. No reproduction may be made, whether by photocopying or by any other means, unless a licence has been obtained from the publisher or its agent.

Cover images, Pat Greenfield: front *R. montroseanum*; back *R.* 'Falcons Gold'; spine *R.* 'Jack Anderson'; front flap *R. magnificum*.

Opposite: *R. falconeri* ssp. *falconeri*.

Book design: Sublime Design Ltd
Map: Tim Nolan, Blackant Mapping Solutions
Printed in Hong Kong through Colorcraft Ltd, Hong Kong

Big-leaf Rhododendrons
Growing the giants of the genus

Glyn Church & Graham Smith
Photographs Pat Greenfield

Bateman

Contents

Foreword by Steve Hootman 6
Key big-leaf rhododendron areas in Central Asia 8
Introduction 10

CHAPTER 1: Big-leafs — where they come from and where
to find them in the wild 15

CHAPTER 2: How rhododendrons influenced woodland
gardens in Britain and around the world 27

CHAPTER 3: Plant collectors — from early days to the present 33

CHAPTER 4: Falconera subsection 49

CHAPTER 5: Grandia subsection 75

CHAPTER 6: Hybrids 101

CHAPTER 7: Where to find them — rhododendron gardens
around the world 113

CHAPTER 8: Growing rhododendrons successfully 133

CHAPTER 9: Propagating rhododendrons 145

CHAPTER 10: Placement and companion plants 153

CHAPTER 11: Conservation — what we can do to save the
giant rhododendrons from extinction 165

Glossary 174
Bibliography 175
Photographic credits 176
With thanks 177
Index 178
The authors 183

Cardiocrinum giganteum at Pukeiti Rhododendron Trust, New Zealand (above), and *R. protistum* 'Pukeiti' in full bloom at Pukeiti with a giant rata behind (opposite).

Foreword

The benign climate of New Zealand provides the perfect conditions for cultivating an incredibly wide range of plant material from around the world. Among the most magnificent and eye-catching of these are the large-leaf *Rhododendron* species. Representing subsections Falconera and Grandia, these are the giants of the genus with some species forming trees up to 30 meters in height. Their often massive, and always impressive leaves, are complemented by the size and glowing beauty of their flowers in shades of white, yellow or pink.

These thirty or so species, native to the temperate rain-forests and subalpine coniferous forests of the Himalaya Mountains, nearby western China and adjacent northern Vietnam, find the conditions under cultivation in New Zealand to be almost perfect. This fine book results from the collaborative efforts of two of the finest plantsmen in New Zealand, Graham Smith and Glyn Church. Graham and Glyn have decades of experience with rhododendrons and large-leaf species in particular and have had many opportunities to study these species both in cultivation and in their native wild habitats.

This beautifully produced volume provides descriptions of these very same habitats along with useful descriptions of each species and the history of its introduction. The tips for successful cultivation gleaned from their years of personal experience growing each of these species is an added bonus for the gardener. In addition to the great color images, many taken in the wild, they describe the best forms of each species.

R. arizelum.

I have been very lucky to have had the opportunity to see the majority of these large-leaf species in the wild and over the years have become more and more fascinated with them as we continue to expand our knowledge of this incredibly diverse, but always beautiful, group of plants. Some of my fondest memories in the field are the times spent hiking along some rough hunter's track through a forest of large-leaf rhododendrons, their massive leaves forming a dense canopy high overhead with only the occasional birdsong breaking the majestic solitude.

Perhaps the most exciting feature of this new treatise is the inclusion of species that are relatively new to our gardens and little-known outside of major collections. Due to ongoing plant exploration into remote and previously unexplored regions of the Sino-Himalaya, there have been several new species of big-leaf rhododendron scientifically documented in recent years for the very first time, their existence on the planet previously completely unknown to botanists and horticulturists. If 30 meter tall flowering trees have remained hidden from the prying eyes of humans for all of these years, one wonders what other treasures remain to be found in the wilds of the world!

Readers will find *Big-leaf Rhododendrons: Growing the Giants of the Genus* to be an entertaining, educational and unique addition to their horticultural library.

Steve Hootman
Curator & executive director, Rhododendron Species Botanical Garden, Washington State, USA

Introduction

Rhododendrons have always had an aura about them, with a reputation as the elite plants of the garden. This air of quality applies even more to the rhododendrons with enormous leaves, commonly referred to as 'big-leafs': people speak about these big-leaf rhododendrons in hushed tones, as if they were royalty, and perhaps that's just it — the big-leaf rhododendrons *are* seen as plant royalty. At least one of them, *Rhododendron kesangiae*, is named after the former Queen of Bhutan; and *R. rex* was named as the king of the genus.

There are several reasons why rhododendrons were seen as the 'posh' plants of the garden, not least because they are difficult and expensive to propagate, which made them quite scarce, and although this is less true today, with modern propagation methods, it was certainly true in their heyday. Rhododendrons also need acid soils, which again creates a scarcity value as not every region has this type of soil. Another major factor is the fact that their homeland is in the high mountains of the distant Himalayas and any plant from Tibet or Bhutan is immediately steeped in mystery and romance.

As a generalisation, a typical rhododendron is hardy and evergreen and well-adapted to a cold climate. As most cold regions only have conifers as evergreens, having these handsome foliage plants available makes them quite special and puts them on a pedestal. They are also tidy rounded bushes for the most part, adding to their desirability.

Three Graham Smith hybrids at Pukeiti: *R. macabeanum* x *magnificum*.

The craze for rhododendrons began in Britain in the 1720s, partly due to a change in fashion in the stately homes of England to the more informal style of woodland gardens. This new style suited rhododendrons perfectly as, for the most part, the cover trees were deciduous, giving shade in summer, but letting more light in during the winter. A part-shaded environment is ideal for most rhododendrons as it keeps the roots cool and the hot sun off the leaves during the summer months, and also protects them from strong drying winds. Rhododendrons like their roots cool and moist and they don't like regular wind as that dries the soil and stresses the leaves. This craze was also triggered by a huge influx of new American plants discovered by the English naturalist, Mark Catesby, and American botanist, horticulturalist and explorer, John Bartram.

In addition, after Britain lost the America War of Independence (1775–1783), she turned to the east, acquiring new colonies in India and Asia with the push up into the Himalayas giving the British first access to Asian rhododendrons. She also gained a foothold in China because of the 'Opium Wars' and plant collectors often risked life and limb to collect crate loads of seeds there, providing ready access to a good supply of plants to meet the growing demand for rhododendrons in the stately gardens in Britain.

Owners of grand estates in Britain have always used their gardens as a means of impressing their friends. The long avenues and 'rides' of trees symbolised power over humankind and nature. The grottoes, follies and statues demonstrated their superior taste. Likewise these structures displayed the owner's knowledge of times past, as the follies often represented the great empires of Greece and Rome. Statues would tell the story of gods and goddesses. Even concepts such as chastity,

INTRODUCTION

fecundity and plenty could be portrayed by statues and follies and quite simple items, like stone pine cones or pineapples on the pillars of the entranceway, conveyed a message — pine cones portrayed fertility and pineapples represented hospitality.

Many of these grand gardens were designed to be enjoyed from the comfort of a carriage, but as the fashion changed from long rides of deciduous trees to a mixed woodland garden, the focus shifted to the actual plants. Everybody likes to think they have something special and unique so the owners created gardens utilising exotic, attention-grabbing species. Initially they grew plants such as pineapples and night-flowering cacti in orangeries and would even have late-night parties just to display their cacti in flower.

The focus shifted again, however; this time to outdoor plants from far-flung places. The landed gentry could all make the 'grand tour' of Europe taking in the sights of Italy, France and Austria, but to have a rare plant from exotic India or China where few white men had ever been was a real coup.

Rhododendrons were a perfect weapon in this one-upmanship battle; they were new, exotic, had fabulous flowers and, best of all, they looked good all year round. If an ordinary rhododendron with leaves as long as your hand was impressive, then imagine what effect having some with leaves as long as your forearm would have — the bigger the better for impressing your friends with some of the mega-leaf species.

What made the big-leafs even more desirable (in a rather perverse sort of way) is that they were rather difficult and required some skill to grow; and, as they would only grow in the acid-soil regions of Great Britain, this limited where they could be grown successfully. Only places with a mild moist climate were likely to succeed. This is still true today, with the only real exception being the Valley Gardens and Savill Garden in the Windsor Royal Gardens, Berkshire, which have a wonderful collection of big-leaf rhododendrons growing in a less-than-perfect climate with only around 50 cm (or less than 20 in) of rain a year.

The obsession for rhododendrons was initiated when renowned British botanist and explorer Joseph Hooker ventured high up into the Himalayas in 1848 and brought back exciting new specimens and seed for propagation. Soon every style-conscious garden-owner wanted to grow them and while, at first, this was limited to the land-owning upper classes, it led to the possibility that nowadays all of us have the chance of growing these amazing plants in our own gardens. Failing that, we can always see them growing in the wild, or make an effort to help to protect them wherever they grow, either wild or in one of the community gardens which has special interest in rhododendrons.

'Falcons Gold' grown from Scottish seeds, *R. falconeri* x *R. macabeanum* (above), and *R. macabeanum* hybrid, self-sown at Pukeiti (opposite).

CHAPTER 1

Big-leafs — where they come from and where to find them in the wild

The first cultivated rhododendrons came from the European Alps and Asia Minor, until early explorers, such as Mark Catesby and John Bartram, discovered the American rhododendron species. But neither of these groups of rhododendrons really set the plant world alight — they were mere curiosities.

R. sinogrande (above), and *R magnificum* (opposite), both at Pukeiti.

The first major influx of new rhododendron species came from the tropics — the hot and steamy jungles of Borneo and the Philippines — but as very few gardens around the world can grow these subtropical Vireya rhododendrons, they seem to have slipped from notice in modern times. Back in 1822, however, the Scottish botanist William Jack discovered and described *Rhododendron malayanum* growing on Mt Bengkoh in Sumatra, which started a craze for these tender, showy plants.

By the early 1840s English collectors were also scouring the Pacific for these Vireya rhododendrons. The large, family-run Veitch Nurseries, in particular, had the down-to-earth Cornishman Thomas Lobb collecting these novelty rhododendrons typified by their plastic-like leaves and waxy flowers. Being frost-tender, they needed special care, but that was no problem for the wealthy estates of England, blessed as they were with glass-walled orangeries and teams of gardeners to tend their exotic plants.

It was, however, the Himalayan rhododendrons that really changed the face of gardening. The first serious collector was William Griffith (1810–1845), but he had no great impact on gardeners as he concentrated on the botanical side of things rather than introducing species

Abies densa forest with rhododendrons in Bhutan.

for cultivation. Griffith was a physician turned botanist employed by the East India Company and later became head of the Calcutta Botanic Garden. Nathaniel Wallich (1786–1854), a Dane in the employ of the East India Company, and Thomas Booth (1829–?), an English amateur, also collected, but it was really Joseph Hooker who changed the way we look at rhododendrons when he ventured into the Himalayas in 1848. By chance he was in the right region to find the huge leaf versions of the genus, the Grandia and Falconera series of big-leaf rhododendrons, and it was from this early start that British gardeners began trying to establish the giant rhododendrons for the estate owners.

High up in the Himalayas, these regal rhododendrons are frequently provided with a high canopy of shade by *Tsuga*, *Abies*, *Picea* or perhaps tall birches, which keeps the plants cooler and protects them from the hot sun. These cool mountain sites are also generally on poorer soils with minimal organic matter, which allows the rhododendrons to compete with other plants. Despite this poor diet, they are able to grow quite well, often forming pure stands in the understorey with only mosses and lichens for company. If conditions were easier and other plants thrived, the rhododendrons may well struggle to compete against the more luxuriant growth.

It's common knowledge that rhododendrons need acid soil and yet in the wild, in areas such as Lijiang in China or parts of Tibet, the natural soil they grow in is limestone, although not the usual soft, friable limestone but a much more durable form called dolomite. Many rhododendrons in the wild are also growing as semi-epiphytes with their roots in a mass of moss and dead organic matter situated on top of the rocky slopes. Usually these plants need lots of moisture, which in these locations comes from snowmelt in the spring and, later, from the summer monsoons.

Another crucial factor is the aspect of the slope to the sun and also to prevailing winds bringing rain. In northern Yunnan, rhododendrons grow mostly on north and northeast-facing slopes, which are cooler and wetter, whereas in southern Yunnan, they frequent the western flanks with plentiful rain and abhor the dry eastern-facing slopes. Further along the Himalayas in Nepal, the north and west-facing slopes have the lush vegetation while the south and east-facing slopes are in constant drought mode. The eastern side of Nepal is much wetter and it gets progressively drier as you go to the west, and it's at a point about midway between east and west that big-leaf rhododendrons cease to grow.

We can study books and notes by plant collectors to determine the orientation of the slopes bearing our favourite rhododendron, but it's all to no avail unless we consider which direction the rain comes from. Many of those high mountain ridges are so steep, the side with the rain can support lush, almost tropical vegetation whereas just over the ridge, it's dust-dry desert; other ridges grow plants at the top where the mountain intercepts the rain but lower down the slope it's semi-arid.

But it's not just the climate or the plants; we're also fascinated by the regions they grow in. From 1850 through to the 1950s, Westerners were fascinated by Tibet, Burma (now Myanmar) and Bhutan and any plants from these hidden kingdoms were doubly valued.

Growing rhododendrons is a well-recognised passion, but once you step into the world of big-leaf or tree rhododendrons it can become an obsession for many. Often people who work in botanic gardens or with large private plant collections find themselves more and more attracted to wild plants rather than cultivated hybrids. There's something quite mesmerising about species from the wild as they have more subtlety and charm than showy cultivars and, of course, more history, too. This is true be it of tiny orchids or massive rhododendron trees.

Once hooked on these beauties it becomes compulsive and you'll find yourself wanting to see them in the wild. While it is fantastic to see magnificent tree rhododendrons in a cultivated collection, there is nothing to compare with the thrill of seeing them in the wild, and it's not just a matter of being able to see the conditions that they grow in naturally, but more a case of the thrill of the chase. Perhaps it can be compared to seeing a tiger in the jungle —it's a special privilege. And for tree rhododendrons, don't put it off as their natural habitat is disappearing fast, year on year.

The pressure on habitat comes mainly from forestry and logging: it could be that the massive *Abies* and *Tsuga* are suitable for logging and that the rhododendrons are 'collateral damage'. Local people also chop them down for fuel and firewood or for slash-and-burn agriculture. Other stresses come from ignorance of their value to the world; local people may choose them as the right timber to build a house and who can blame them if they have always lived with these

R. rex ssp. *rex* and *R. heliolepos* var. *fumidum* with mauve flowers at Yaoshan, north-east Yunnan.

trees on their doorstep? Back in 1901, Ernest Wilson was sent to China by Veitch Nurseries to find the *Davidia* or handkerchief tree. Following Augustine Henry's detailed description of the location, he made his way to the valley and the actual spot where the tree should be. All he found was a stump and a newly built but rather ramshackle house beside it. The locals had chopped down the tree and made themselves a brand-new dwelling. It took him weeks to find some more handkerchief trees.

Worse destruction was to come in China in the 1960s and '70s when Chairman Mao had the bright idea of melting down second-hand metal to make new steel. All they succeeded in doing was to decimate vast areas of forest to fuel the fires in order to make second-rate pig iron. In the process, many magnificent trees were lost, including whole hillsides of rhododendrons and, of course, much of the forest containing the big-leaf and tree rhododendrons. It is impossible to replace this virgin forest, and so all we can do is hope to preserve what still exists in the Himalayas. The situation is very good in both Sikkim and Bhutan, but in virtually every other region the remaining forest is severely threatened. By lucky chance, the situation in Arunachal Pradesh is improving all the time and much of the forest there remains untouched. Because the younger generation are keen to move to the cities, the remaining farmers do not need to put pressure on the forest; many of them are also moving down to lower altitudes, replacing those who have shifted to the city.

On the plus side of the equation, it's now easier than ever for the ordinary traveller to get to remote areas and find big-tree rhododendrons. Many large gardens and botanical organisations run regular tours based around giving clients the chance to see plants in the wild, which makes sense as a group can travel for less cost per person than just one or two people can. There are other advantages, too: these tours go to the prime sites and use experts as guides, so you have the twin benefits of their plant expertise and the time saved trying to find the best locations. Finally, and crucially, we all love to share our passions and a group of like-minded people to share your joy and knowledge with is the best company you can have.

R. kesangiae in Bhutan.

As a child I remember my father avidly reading the latest volume from Reginald Farrer (the famous plant collector and rockery doyen) or Francis Kingdon Ward, as he imagined himself in the steamy jungles of Burma. With his book and his pipe, he was snug beside a roaring log fire, trying to picture a forest festooned with fabulous plants, many of which would be unknown in the scientific world and impossible to visualise. People of his generation would never have thought that, within the space of a few decades, it would become so easy to follow in famous collectors' footsteps. Well, perhaps I should qualify that, as there are still areas of northern Burma (Myanmar), or neighbouring Manipur and Nagaland, which are either off-limits or extremely difficult to access. Travellers tell me the Mishmi Hills in Arunachal Pradesh are easier because the people are friendly, although the Naga still have a reputation for being fierce and tend to be a bit rebellious.

Dulong Valley in north-west Yunnan.

CHINA

YUNNAN

Nowadays it's easy to gain access to most of western China. Both Yunnan and Sichuan are fairly easy destinations for the amateur and serious botanist alike. We can all visit Lijiang, a World Heritage site, and next day climb the Yulong Xue Shan, or go to Dali and race up the Cangshan where French missionary and botanist Jean Marie Delavay and George Forrest discovered so much of their treasure. In their day, the ranges were known as the Tali and Lichiang, which explains why so many plants have *taliensis* or *likiangensis* as their species names. Instead of trudging up the mountain, however, these days we can take the cable car up the Cangshan and soon be in country where you can find *Rhododendron rex* spp. *fictolacteum* and *R. taliense*. In the 1940s the eccentric Austrian collector Joseph Rock lived in the Lijiang area studying the plants and the local Naxi language. A remarkable man, he was the first to depict and translate this unusual language which in its writing, uses many symbols or pictograms in conjunction with a more usual script.

George Forrest also worked the mountains to the south. Not far from his base in Tengchong are the Gaoligongshan mountains in the far west of Yunnan. A sizable area of this marvellous mountain range is now a World Heritage site and has *R. protistum*, *R. protistum* var. *giganteum*, *R. rex* ssp. *fictolacteum* and *R. sinogrande* and, hopefully, is preserved forever.

In recent times, in the last thirty years or so there has been much cooperation between the local botanical institutions and gardens in the West. The Kunming Institute of Botany in particular has been outward-looking, forging relationships with like-minded gardens in the West such as Pukeiti in New Zealand, Edinburgh Botanic Gardens and the Rhododendron Species

R. arizelum in north-west Yunnan shaped over time by heavy snow drifts.

Foundation in Seattle. Scientists, like Professor Guan Kaiyun from the Kunming Institute of Botany and former Director of the Kunming Botanic Garden, have been very proactive in saving remnant forests and also in forging links with foreign institutions to aid their cause. It's possible to join tours of these Yunnan forests by contacting Pukeiti and others.

As well as the zones in the north and west of the province where you'd expect to find big-leaf rhodos, there are also pockets of *R. sinofalconeri* in Pingbian county, in the Daweishan Ranges near the Vietnam border. This area is now a nature reserve so we can expect to see the forest preserved for future generations to enjoy.

To quote the late Peter Wharton, formerly curator of the David C. Lam Asian Garden at the University of British Columbia Botanical Garden:

> *We returned to Gongshan to prepare for our second major objective, a 4-day field exploration of the Qiqi Pass. The Qiqi is famous for the presence of the rare and endangered conifer* Taiwania flousiana, *a close relative of the Sierra redwood. It occurs in small, scattered stands within dense broadleaved forests at 2000–2200 m. Mature trees rise to over 60 m and tower above the surrounding forest. We saw life zones from sub-tropical to subalpine, all of which impressed me with their extraordinary floristic diversity. Massive trees of* Rhododendron protistum *and* R. sinogrande *grow to over 20 m in some localities. Again, I was heartened by the knowledge that these priceless forests are revered and are to be conserved for posterity.*

SICHUAN

While Sichuan offers a treasure-trove of plants, it's not the best place in the world to be seeking big-leaf rhododendrons. *R. galactinum*, *R. rex* ssp. *rex* and *R. watsonii* are found here, but unless you're a fanatic you're unlikely to be impressed.

Since the late 1950s the area to the west has been incorporated into Sichuan. What was previously the Tibetan region of Muli and Ganze is now part of Sichuan. Likewise, the Deqin area of north Yunnan was previously part of Tibet and the local people are all Tibetan. Since the takeover there has been a huge influx of Han Chinese into these regions. From a plant point of view, this is exciting because it is part of the area described as south-east Tibet by Kingdon Ward and others. However, because of sensitivities over Tibet, a lot of these areas are hard to access.

BIG-LEAF RHODODENDRONS

XIZANG, AUTONOMOUS REGION FORMERLY KNOWN AS TIBET

In recent times the Chinese authorities have been happy for foreigners to visit Tibet providing it's in the areas they designate as suitable. The new rail link from Beijing to Lhasa, with its staggering use of technology to overcome the problem of having to have rails situated on permafrost, has genuinely opened up Tibet to a stream of tourists. Lhasa, or Gyantse, are easily accessible, but while this is good for tourists of Tibetan culture and architecture, it's not very exciting from the point of view of plants people, other than lovers of alpines. Those who want to see hillsides of rhododendrons, or big-leaf trees, will have to travel further as most of these grow in the south-east of the country. As mentioned, some of the forested area is now enclosed in Yunnan and Sichuan. Much of these regions is still officially off limits and likely to remain so, in which case it may be some time before you can follow in the footsteps of Joseph Rock and Kingdon Ward. However, this means no tourists or any others for that matter, in which case it's likely that our favourite rhododendrons will be left to live in peaceful contentment for the foreseeable future.

In north-west Yunnan you're allowed as far as Deqin, which is in a Tibetan region, but access is denied to anyone wanting to go north from here. From a plant perspective, especially for trees, shrubs and rhododendrons, the exciting bit is the south-east of the country, and in neighbouring Myanmar and Arunachal Pradesh in India. Because these national boundaries are still disputed it's nigh on impossible to get into this part of Tibet unless you sneak across the border from the south. Don't expect a gunboat rescue if you get caught! Some intrepid collectors have, in fact, ventured seemingly unnoticed and without making a fuss about it into these regions in the last thirty years.

R. sinogrande trunk hosting a good crop of epiphytes and hanging orchids.

VIETNAM

A few years ago no one would have included Vietnam in a list of nations with big-leaf rhododendrons. Following the opening up of the country and their willingness to host tourists, plant enthusiasts have been surprised to find many exciting rhododendron species growing here. The mountains in the north above Hanoi and near the Chinese border are technically part of the Himalayas. But apart from a few transitory botanists such as Irish plantsman and sinologist Augustine Henry, no one had really thought to study this area. Now, it appears, thanks to the likes of Tom Hudson, Keith Rushforth and Alan Clark, we know there are pockets of rhododendrons in the far north.

So far only two large-leaved species have been found in Vietnam — *R. sinofalconeri* and *R. suoilenhense*. As far as we know, *R. sinofalconeri* only occurs around the Sapa area on Fansipan mountain south of the Red River. At 10,312 ft (3143 m) Mt Fansipan is the highest peak in the country, situated very near the Chinese border, roughly midway east to west of the country.

R. suoilenhense in the Grandia section was found on Mt Suilen, which again is near Sapa, and also in other areas in the Hoang Lien Son mountains. As well, there is a population on Mt Tay Con Linh, 8583 ft (2616 m), which is north and east of the Red River. They both grow at a slightly lower altitude of around 7400–7800 ft (2250–2400 m) alongside *Tsuga dumosa*, and members of the Fagaceae and Lauraceae families as the main forest constituents.

BURMA OR MYANMAR

While Tibet is mostly offlimits, northern Burma has been even more difficult to access. North Burma is currently an impossible area to visit unless you're willing to take the risk of walking from village to village after crossing the border from India or China. It is possible, but very dangerous. My wife Gail and I travelled into parts of eastern Burma in the 1980s without the authorities knowing, simply by turning up and being non-threatening. Naturally a few bribes had to change hands as well.

These areas were not especially easy to visit back in Kingdon Ward's day either, although back then at least it was technically British even if the inhabitants had no idea where or what Britain was, and in theory they would send a search party if anything happened to you. The only problem was, by the time news of your demise reached the authorities, your carcass would probably be unrecognisable!

R. sinogrande, Hpimaw Pass, northern Myanmar (top) and Trongsa in central Bhutan (bottom).

ARUNACHAL PRADESH

This Indian state contains uncharted forests and new plants are being discovered all the time. For instance Kenneth Cox discovered *R. titapuriense* here in 2005. Some of the *R. titapuriense* trees discovered are 90 ft (27 m) in height. To think such massive plants were previously unknown gives some indication of how remote and unexplored this region is. In India there are an estimated 90 species of rhododendron and two thirds of these are found in Arunachal Pradesh. Botanical tourism is possible, but it's not easy and not for the faint-hearted.

Apart from William Griffith and Kingdon Ward, few plant hunters have traversed these hills until very recent times with intrepid collectors, such as Kenneth Cox, Steve Hootman, Tom Hudson, Keith Rushforth and others, discovering all sorts of plant treasure from this region, including *R. mechukae*.

BIG-LEAF RHODODENDRONS

ASSAM, NAGALAND AND MANIPUR

All three of these areas in north-east India are difficult to access. Until recently, William Griffith and Kingdon Ward were our only sources for plant material from these remote regions. However, the rewards are high if you do venture here as these areas have not been fully explored. Steve Hootman of the Rhododendron Species Foundation in Seattle and other modern collectors have been retracing the steps of those early collectors.

BHUTAN

After years of being hidden away, Bhutan is much more accessible these days. They do limit the number of tourists and, very wisely, they charge a set fee per day, regardless of accommodation standard. The idea behind the policy is that their infrastructure can only cope with a certain number of tourists and if everyone only paid the actual local costs, then the country would not really benefit. If every tourist pays a levy, this revenue is available to pay for better roads and education.

The experience is so incredible it's worth the extra cost. I've yet to meet a tourist who resented this extra charge; we Westerners can easily afford this money to improve the lives of the Bhutanese people and, in most cases, it actually makes visitors feel good once the policy is explained and you realise some of your tourist dollars will go directly towards improving the lives and education of these wonderful people.

Bhutan is truly the last piece of paradise. Over 70 per cent of its forest is intact and in the same condition as when Joseph Hooker was travelling in the Himalayas back in 1850. Thankfully they have an ongoing policy of preserving their forests. Bhutan has also managed to keep its culture intact — more what the Tibetans dream of, than that in the current Sino Tibet. Recently, Bhutan has been getting worldwide publicity for regarding the 'Gross Domestic Happiness' as more important than 'Gross Domestic Product', as we do in the West. In other words, happiness is worth more than money. Even the British Prime Minister has lauded the Bhutanese approach to life and held it up as a model to follow.

To me Bhutan is perfection, the best country I have ever visited. From a purely botanical point of view it is exquisite

Prayer flags (top) and *R. kesangiae* (bottom), Bhutan.

R. hodgsonii in Yumthang Valley, Sikkim.

because so much of the native forest is still intact and untouched by human hand. From the point of view of rhododendrons, however, you're unlikely to encounter whole hillsides as you do in Nepal or China; it's more a case of one here and one there, but you come across more as you travel further east. The highlight is undoubtedly the large drifts of *R. kesangiae* on Pele La and Dochu La and you can also find *R. falconeri*, *R. grande*, *R. hodgsonii*, and the occasional *R. griffithianum* there.

The Bhutanese government has recently established a new semi-natural collection of rhododendrons and other native plants at Serbithang south of the capital Thimphu.

SIKKIM

This Indian state is where it all began with Joseph Hooker in 1849, so if you want to follow in Hooker's footsteps then here's your chance. Sikkim is fairly easy to visit and the roads, infrastructure and accommodation are all quite adequate.

Keshab Pradhan, who recently gained a Royal Horticultural Society honour, the Veitch Memorial Medal, has written a delightful handbook: *The Rhododendrons of Sikkim* published in 2010 by Sikkim Adventure Botanical Tours and Treks, www.sikkim-adventure.com. Keshab and his family are the best source of information for seeking rhododendrons in Sikkim.

R. falconeri, *R. grande* and *R. hodgsonii* are all easily found and quite common in places. Tsomgo Lake just 40 km from the capital Gangtok is a good region to view them.

Singalila National Park in the west of the country in the state of West Bengal (India) and right on the Nepalese border is another perfect location for finding big-leaf rhododendrons growing in temperate forest. Invariably the *R. grande* are at the lowest altitude, then Dr Falconer's *R. falconeri* with Hodgson's rhododendron *R. hodgsonii* at the highest altitude. There is of course some overlapping between the species. There are many other species of rhododendron in Sikkim.

NEPAL

Nepal is one of the easier countries to travel to and a very rewarding destination. There are lots of well-organised tours to see the native habitat, either by minibus or by trekking. Language is not a problem and the people are very friendly and welcoming.

You will see whole hillsides of *R. arboreum* in some areas. Nepal is rightly famous for rhododendrons en masse covering acres of mountainside, with species such as *R. campanulatum*, *R. barbatum*, *R. cinnabarinum* and *R. thomsonii*. Unfortunately, there is lots of deforestation in Nepal because of the pressure of a high population and people chopping down the trees for fuel and firewood.

If you're specifically looking for big-leafs, they are found in the east of the country. *R. falconeri* grows around the Kachenjunga area; *R. hodgsonii* is more widespread and as always found at higher altitudes over 9843 ft (3000 m). *R. grande* is not uncommon and found at lower altitudes in the east of the country.

R. grande at Barsey, Sikkim (left) and *R. arboreum* (right) in Nepal.

BIG-LEAFS — WHERE THEY COME FROM AND WHERE TO FIND THEM IN THE WILD

CHAPTER 2

How rhododendrons influenced woodland gardens in Britain and around the world

During the 1860s, a number of French missionaries based in China began sending plants home to France, but other than a small coterie of fanatics this made little impact on the world of gardening, especially as they mostly sent dried specimens rather than seeds or actual plants.

The transformational era of the plant hunter began in the new century with George Forrest. In those halcyon days during the first three decades of the twentieth century such was the flood of new plants from China, Tibet and Burma that the gardens of expedition shareholders began to burst at the seams. In many ways, the gardeners of Britain were surprised so many of these new plants were hardy. British gardeners have always held the suspicion that all plants from exotic locations must be tender. This was borne out by descriptions in old editions of *The RHS Manual* and *Sanders Encyclopaedia* where virtually every plant from an exotic locale was listed as tender.

Arduaine Garden, Oban, Scotland with *Davidia involucrata* (Dove Tree) in the foreground.

During the years of the great collectors, the vast majority of plants seemed to be alpine treasures or else rhododendrons. The rhododendrons are the real legacy of this fantastic era because it's hard to sustain exotics like primulas and gentians over a period of decades. And, fortunately, most of these precious rhododendrons turned out to be hardy or near enough hardy to tempt friends and fellow collectors to try growing them. Rhododendrons became the new orchids, the new craze all through the first half of the nineteenth century and most of the second half. Rhododendrons were synonymous with taste and discernment.

How did this come about? Primarily it was to do with empire building. Interestingly, the fashion for woodland gardens was born out of the colonisation of America and reached fruition with the prising open of China's borders.

Between 1720 and 1760, the number of plants grown in English gardens increased five-fold. Most of these new plants came from the American colonies and included the first exotic rhododendrons. So began a new trend: formality and straight lines were passé and informal plantings based on New World plants came into vogue. The idea was to construct a garden that replicated nature and negated the hand of man, which was in complete contrast to the heavy-handed formal gardens of the day.

This soft natural woodland look became the norm for the big estates in England, and although we think of Lancelot 'Capability' Brown (1716–1783) as the master of this style, he was, in fact, to come much later. The true founders were William Kent (1685–1748) and Charles Bridgeman (1690–1738). Bridgeman, with the title of 'Royal Gardener', had help from William Kent to redesign the gardens at Richmond Park near Windsor, Kensington Palace, Hampton Court, Hyde Park and Kew for the Royal family.

Bridgeman's gardens retained the formal gardens immediately surrounding the house but then, as one moved further away, became more and more informal. He was the first to use the ha-ha in an English garden, to incorporate distant meadows into the estate owner's view.

William Kent also liked ha-has and designed very informal gardens. Originally an artist, he was encouraged to create gardens like paintings by his patron Richard Boyle (1694–1753), the Third Earl of Burlington (also Fourth Earl of Cork). Richard Boyle, who owned the Londesborough estate in Yorkshire and Chiswick House near London, was a leading light in the new trend. Recognised now as the man who 'discovered' Kent's talent, he was pivotal as a leader of fashion.

Kent went on to design the inspirational garden at Stowe near Oxford, owned by Viscount Cobham, Sir Richard Temple. This garden, both then and now, is seen as the epitome of style, portraying nature in a positive way. As Horace Walpole, politician and gardening authority, said of Kent, 'He leaped the fence and saw that all nature was a garden'.

This whole movement towards creating a natural garden came about because of a huge influx of new plants, including rhododendrons, mostly from the American colonies of Virginia and Carolina introduced by the likes of Mark Catesby and John Bartram. The plants they sent home included the first magnolias, and hydrangeas grown in Western gardens. The collections

Pink *R. falconeri* ssp. *eximium* and yellow *R. arizelum* at Stonefield Castle, Scotland.

also included exciting new rhododendrons to add to the few European and Asia Minor species already being grown.

When Britain lost control of America after the War of Independence, she turned her eyes to the East, and what started as a trading battle with the Dutch for access to spices ended up with Britain acquiring new territories. In part, this was due to private companies like the East India Company taking over huge swathes of land in and around India.

Britain also gained a foothold in China and instigated the Opium Wars to secure more trade and power. At each subsequent treaty, Britain demanded more and more benefits of trade, and also freedom of movement for missionaries and plant hunters. The French sent missionaries, many of them part-time plant collectors, but Britain cut to the chase and sent full-time plant hunters.

When the Asiatic rhododendrons came on the scene it was perfect timing as the new woodland gardens suited them perfectly. Trees planted 100 or more years previously were reaching maturity and provided the ideal foil and shade canopy for the new plants. They protected the rhododendrons from the hot summer sun and also from strong gales and drying winds. It's hard to imagine rhododendrons ever becoming so well established in these estate gardens without this existing tree canopy. So, all in all, it was the perfect match.

It was also unlikely that the existing rhododendrons from America, Europe and Turkey would, in themselves, ever be sufficient to create a new fashion, but the never-ending supply from Asia was like a river of gold. An inkling of what was to come began first with Robert Fortune, and then Jean Marie Delavay, collecting in China, but it was the trio of Forrest, Ward and Wilson and

Gardens at Arduaine, Scotland.

the support of well-heeled folk such as Arthur Bulley and J.C. Williams who really gave impetus to the new garden style. It wasn't long before the fashion spread to other estate owners. Arthur Bulley, a rich cotton merchant from Lancashire, England, became so passionate about plants he began his own seed company, Bees Ltd, in 1904. J.C. Williams resided at Caerhays Castle in Cornwall where he improved the plant collection there immensely by funding George Forrest and other collectors.

In any society, gardeners know each other and swap plants among themselves, and although there is often a slightly competitive edge, if one gives a friend a new plant, you can both make comparisons over the years, as they grow. And for ordinary folk to emulate the landed gentry and have a rhododendron or two in their own gardens was a talking point with certain bragging rights.

After the First World War there was a feeling of freedom as less people worked on estates and more worked in factories or for government departments, such as the railways. Those in the emerging middle class could afford a house with a decorative garden and while they might begin planting vegetables and annuals, inevitably they would want the more fashionable plants, and that included rhododendrons. Magazines and seed merchants who catered to this new, aspiring generation encouraged this fashion for gardens. Arthur Bulley of Bees Ltd seed company seized the opportunity to import new and novel plants for the masses.

The general populace also picks up on things that seize their imaginations and because there was such a wide variety of rhododendrons, this made them a logical and rewarding choice.

Rhododendrons kept their high profile pretty much throughout the twentieth century, and it was only when improved propagation techniques resulted in falling prices that the novelty wore off somewhat.

Part of the mystique of rhododendrons, which adds to their desirability, is that they only grow on acid soils and this discounted the vast swathes of Britain where chalk and limestone dominate. Their propagation was tricky, too, and that kept them rather scarce. They could be grown from seed but only those in the loop were likely to receive any. Seed from garden plants would not 'come true' because they would hybridise with all the neighbouring plants, and so were not worthwhile. Propagation from cuttings was difficult and surrounded in mystery in a way that only old-time English gardeners could take pleasure in. A new entrant would have to train for seven years and, even then, not expect to be told all the secrets by old hands for another decade or so. The simple way to propagate them was by layering, as virtually every rhododendron can be propagated by layers, and no doubt the more generous souls did pass on their plant treasures in this way.

As the twentieth century progressed, many of the rich estates fell on hard times, especially after the Second World War with the introduction of death duties, and some owners resorted to opening their stately homes to the general public. Once cars became more common, places like Longleat and Stourhead enjoyed huge queues of visitors every weekend. These new tourists were naturally inspired to imitate the gardens they saw and the dominant plants at eye level were often rhododendrons.

This flourishing fashion for rhododendrons was emulated in America and around the British Empire, wherever climate allowed. On the east coast of America the trend was biased towards mass plantings of azaleas and rhododendrons as seen on many golf courses and large gardens like the Biltmore in North Carolina. West coast America came to rhododendrons in the latter half of the twentieth century and was based around avid collectors rather than estates. The cooler coastal areas of Australia, and especially Tasmania, are suited to rhododendrons cultivation; the inland hilly regions with sufficient rainfall are particularly ideal.

New Zealand is seen by many as perfect rhododendron country with a range of climates but generally mild and often wet. This small country boasts the full gambit of continental climates and so virtually every temperate plant can be grown somewhere in the country. With the predominant winds from the north and the west, it's natural the west coast gardens grow them to perfection, but there are also several notable collections on the east side of both main islands.

CHAPTER 3

Plant collectors — from early days to the present

The craze for rhododendrons was triggered when Joseph Hooker ventured high up into the Himalayas in 1848 and appeared to come to an end around 1958 when Frank Kingdon Ward died.

But we are in a new era with several keen men scouring the mountains of far-flung places to find big-leaf rhododendrons. Notable among them are Steve Hootman, Tom Hudson, Keith Rushforth, Kenneth Cox and Alan Clark. To everyone's surprise they are discovering many new species, though it may take years to sort them all out because, as we know, big-leaf rhododendrons can take decades to flower.

R. sinogrande at Pukeiti (above), and *R. falconeri* ssp. *falconeri*, 150-year-old Joseph Hooker seedling, Stonefield Castle in Scotland (opposite).

SIR JOSEPH HOOKER 1817–1911

The man who began the craze for rhododendrons was Joseph Hooker. As a young man, Joseph had a wanderlust and a desperate desire to see the world. His father suggested he become a surgeon as this would allow him to travel in someone's employ. Then, having qualified, he enrolled as an assistant surgeon on the Ross voyage to Antarctica. But Joseph really wanted was to study plants full-time, so he quit the navy and with the help of Lord Auckland and his father at Kew, he managed to get his dream job, studying the flora and fossils of the Himalayas. In April 1848, he arrived in Darjeeling, then a part of Sikkim, a beautiful region in the hills with that rare commodity in British India, a pleasant, cool climate. Ensconced in a piece of heaven, he enjoyed a blissful stay with Brian Hodgson (1800–1894), an eccentric retired diplomat who studied local birds and animals. Hodgson was a fount of knowledge regarding the geography, local tribes and customs as well as natural history of the area. One of the first plants Hooker named was the fabulous *Rhododendron hodgsonii* for his friend and mentor.

R. hodgsonii trunk, at Baravalla, Scotland (left); Joseph Hooker (middle); and *R. hodgsonii*, painting from Hooker's book, *The Rhododendrons of Sikkim*, 1841 (right).

Hooker then teamed up with Dr Archibald Campbell (1805–1874), the British Political Agent in Darjeeling. Two men looking for adventure, they set off to explore the country and were hopeful of meeting the Sikkimese Rajah. Apart from a minor skirmish when Campbell was taken hostage, they had a wonderful time. Hooker, being a loyal friend, refused to desert him, so was still around when he was finally released and they continued their travels together. (The upshot of Campbell's incarceration was that, in retaliation, Britain annexed Darjeeling.)

Their adventure wasn't in vain from a botanical standpoint either. Hooker managed to collect seeds and plants of literally dozens of rhododendrons while he was high up in the Himalayas. These new plants sparked a whole new craze which continues to this day. Being a generous man, Hooker named his discoveries after his friends and so we have *Rhododendron thomsonii* and *R. falconeri* as well as *Magnolia campbellii*. He also brought back *R. grande* named as *R. argenteum*.

Joseph Hooker undertook another expedition from May to December 1850 to the Khasia Hills in north-east India with a friend, Dr Thomas Thomson. After this he returned to England and continued to study botany, sometimes in tandem with Charles Darwin, a life-long friend. The two men frequently worked together trying to fathom out how plants adapt to their environment, and both men contributed to the theory of evolution. A true friend, Hooker was the first scientist to publicly back Darwin when he published his *Origin of the Species*. This was probably a riskier and braver action than sailing through Antarctic waters in a flimsy wooden ship, as the press had a field day attacking both men.

Hooker was a back-room boffin and always happier when working outdoors or doing some private study; he wasn't at ease in company or being centre stage. One time he wrote to Darwin saying he dreaded the thought of following his father as Director of Kew, but that's exactly what he did. Subsequently, he also became President of the Royal Society. In later years he was knighted for services to botany, but he declined the honour because it wasn't for services to India. Following the publication of his *Flora of British India* he was, however, then knighted for services to India.

WILLIAM GRIFFITH 1810–1845

William Griffith is the forgotten hero of Himalayan plant exploration. It seems every second plant in northern India and especially Bhutan is named after him. Although Joseph Hooker gets the credit as the first rhododendron man in the Himalayas, Griffith was there collecting thirteen years before him. The reason he isn't acknowledged is because he didn't publish or get round to actually naming a lot of the plants he found. His long-term plan was to discover and catalogue as many plants as possible from all across the Indian continent and beyond and then retire to England to classify and publish his findings.

Between 1832 and his death in 1845 he botanised across much of India, Assam, Afghanistan, modern day Pakistan, Burma and Bhutan. His tour of duty as surgeon on Major Pemberton's embassy to Bhutan allowed him to botanise through this incredibly remote and beautiful plant paradise. As part of the British East India Company, the de facto British army, he had the huge advantage of coolies to carry his plants and belongings as they traversed most of Bhutan from east to west, from Tashigang to Thimpu, and back down to India through the subtropical region.

On the high passes, Griffith found lots of big-leaf rhododendrons but it's hard to make sense of what he found. Naturally he couldn't know everything about everything, and so he described

R. falconeri, painting from Hooker's book on the rhododendrons of Sikkim, 1841 (left); William Griffith (middle), who may have been the first botanist to see many of the big-leaf rhododendrons in the wild, including *R. falconeri*; and *R. falconeri* (right).

many plants in the old way with multiple Latin names. The Bhutan trip began in mid-1837, ending back in Calcutta in June 1839. After botanising through Bhutan he wrote to Robert Wight, Scottish surgeon and botanist: 'Of the Rhododendrons, I cannot speak in terms of sufficient ecstasy. I have upwards of 15 species, which number might perhaps be doubled by a longer residence.'

Griffith was given various postings around India, then sent to Afghanistan with the invading British army during the First Afghan War 1839–1942 but he was too ill with dysentery to remain, and was dispatched back to India before the army's crushing defeat. When sufficiently recovered from his exertions, he was given a medical post at Malacca. Shortly afterwards, in September 1844, he married a Miss Henderson. But their happiness was short lived as he died in Malacca on 9 February 1845.

A man with diverse tastes, he noticed and collected every wayside weed including ferns, liverworts and mosses. He was also interested in morphology and studied the vessels and ovaries of plants. In his correspondence with Robert Wight it's obvious he had a grand scheme to change the face of botany. He saw the plant world in flux and thought the idea of fixed species and even genera as too rigid, intending to incorporate subgenera and subspecies.

Because Griffith died such a young man, there was no time to bring his plans to fruition. We can only imagine what he may have achieved had he lived to a ripe old age. Today we remember him for the heavenly scented *Rhododendron griffithianum*, but it's likely he was the first botanist to set eyes on *R. hodgsonii*, *R. falconeri*, *R. grande* and *R. kesangiae*.

JEAN MARIE DELAVAY 1834–1895

Plant hunting was never a competition, though it was competitive at times, especially when money or ego were involved. Had it ever been a contest then Jean Marie Delavay would have been way out in front. George Forrest subsequently claimed the Delavay territory in north-west Yunnan and got the credit for many plants first seen by this quiet missionary. Forrest, with his huge teams of local workers, collected in the region of 30,000 pressed specimens while Delavay collected over 200,000 on his own. Delavay's specimens gathered dust in the Paris museums and were forgotten and so he does not get the credit for discovering many of the more than 4000 different species he found in China. At least 1500 of these were thought to be new to science, some say as many as 2500. It's an astonishing achievement.

Initially, he was stationed near the coast and collected plants for Dr Henry Hance, a member of the British Consulate. But during his next posting near Dali in north-west Yunnan he was persuaded to send his specimens to Paris under the care of Adrien Franchet. This new base was perfect — a dry warm valley, and therefore a healthy place to live, and situated between two huge mountain ranges simply covered in wondrous plants. It must have been heaven for him, with hundreds of plants waiting to be discovered.

The surprising thing about Delavay's collecting is that it was only a sideline, a hobby, a passionate one no less but he still had to fulfil his missionary duties. Franchet described his pressed specimens as the best he'd ever seen and not only were they sent in vast numbers, but he often managed to get flowers and seed capsules on the same specimen page by revisiting the area and completing the botanical picture. His descriptions and notes were very thorough, too. Very few others ever had the time or energy to complete such a task.

Delavay must have been the first European to see the blue poppy *Meconopsis betonicifolia*. Many glorious plants were named after him with the epithet 'delavayi' including aster, *Incarvillea*, iris, magnolia, *Osmanthus*, *Paeonia* and, of course, the gorgeous *Rhododendron delavayi*, as well as various big-leaf rhododendrons such as *R. fictolacteum* and *R. sinogrande*.

Having combed the local mountains, Delavay decided to go further afield and climb the Likiang ranges peaking at about 23,000 ft (7000 m). It proved to be his downfall; the route was difficult, and the weather even worse. Tragically he was struck down by bubonic plague and although he survived, his left arm was paralysed. Thereafter his health was always a concern. The following year he made another attempt on Likiang but a combination of bad weather and poor health prevented him scaling the heights he hoped. So in the autumn of 1891 he sailed home and lived comfortably in a sanatorium in the south of France. But three years later he was back in China, based in north-east Yunnan. The long journey from France, the humid climate, everything was against him, and soon his health was so bad he had to retire to Kunming where he died in December 1895. Why oh why didn't he return to Paris and spend the last decade of his life cataloguing his precious plants or writing a chronicle of his adventures? But who are we to challenge the faith of this loyal cleric, this gentle kindly man who loved his plants, his mountains and his God?

GEORGE FORREST 1873–1932

George Forrest is rightly famous for introducing many novel plants, but he was also responsible for inspiring a new form of gardening. Woodland gardens, with rhododendrons, camellias, *Pieris* and primulas, did not exist before George Forrest went plant hunting. Before his time, there were only a few Himalayan, European and American rhododendrons in cultivation. His haul of new rhododendron species was so great that botanists had to rework the genus. In the old days rhododendrons and azaleas were thought to be two different genera. Forrest's new plants forced the botanists to merge them into one.

In all, he made seven expeditions to western China and got to know the region better than anyone. The first two trips in 1904–7 and 1910–11 were both for Arthur Bulley of Bees Nursery near Liverpool after Forrest had been recommended by Professor Balfour of the Edinburgh Royal Botanic Garden. His instructions were simple; he was told to find commercial garden-worthy plants.

Forrest didn't always get on with Bulley, but got on famously with Balfour who catalogued his collections. From 1911 onwards, Forrest was financed by various syndicates as he specialised more in rhododendrons and primulas. From 1911 to 1915, his sponsors were J.C. Williams of Caerhays in

George Forrest in China.

*Botanists are sometimes categorised as 'lumpers' or 'splitters'. The lumpers think the differences between species are minor and 'lump' two or more species into one. This is commonplace in the field of rhododendrons, while some genera such as Sophora have many new species as the splitters have decided the variations are worthy of specific status and have split one species into four or five new ones.

Cornwall, who was to receive all the rhododendrons, and Reginald Cory of Duffryn, who got all other seeds. Later trips were also funded by syndicates, with J.C. Williams at the top of the list.

During his travels George Forrest collected in the region of 30,000 plant specimens for herbarium collections and a huge number of seed packets and, in the process, discovered over 300 new species of rhododendrons. This vast number of species was later whittled down by botanists 'lumping'* various species into one, and so the figure of 300 may be halved to fit with today's botanical tomes. Either way, it's a truly amazing record.

These remarkable facts and figures give us some idea of what George Forrest did, but what of the man? What inspired him to spend most of his adult life in the company of Chinese peasants collecting seeds and plants? Often described as brusque and a loner, he obviously did enjoy his own company and was not at ease in formal or large gatherings.

His first job on leaving school was with a pharmaceutical chemist. He didn't like it much but he did gain some useful knowledge of drugs and plants. He pined for an outdoor life and when a small legacy came his way he headed for Australia. If he wasn't tough before he went, he certainly was after ten years working in the goldfields and sheep stations in outback Australia.

Returning to Scotland in 1902, a chance meeting with Professor Balfour changed his life. Initially he was given employment as a herbarium assistant, and then the chance to work for Bulley. Forrest had an unusual approach, establishing a base from where he would send out his trained locals in twos and threes to collect seed from plants marked when in flower earlier in the year. The seed harvests were brought back by runners. Forrest was unique among plant collectors with this method of collecting; he was probably the most successful collector ever in terms of introductions, certainly many rhododendron growers will say so. Forrest was a unique character and a man of the people who enjoyed living with the Yunnan peasants whose lifestyle was not dissimilar to that of the Scottish Highlanders. Relating well to local people enabled him to live with and be trusted by them. George Forrest was the kind of man you want in your team when the going gets tough or, as my father would say, the sort of man you'd go hunting tigers with.

AUGUSTINE HENRY 1857–1930

Augustine Henry seemed destined for adventure. His father sought fortune on the goldfields of California and Australia before returning to Ireland where Augustine was born in 1857. A natural scholar, he trained as a physician but he was desperate to travel. Like his father he was looking for adventure and joined the Chinese Customs Service. It seems an unlikely occupation but after the Taiping revolution in the 1850s the Chinese government realised foreign clerics had maintained their role during any local revolts and paid all dues after the turmoil. This realisation led to the formation of a customs service manned by foreign workers who were trustworthy and not open to bribery.

In 1882 he was based in Ichang, a busy inland port way up the Yangtze River. Much of the trade in the city was in medicines made from local plants. While Henry had a medical background he did not have any knowledge of Chinese plants, so he began sending plant specimens to Kew for identification. Kew realised they were onto a good thing, having a man on the spot in China, and so a fruitful correspondence between Henry and Sir Joseph Hooker began. Soon Henry was avidly collecting and pressing plants as well as learning Chinese. Both skills were to become invaluable.

Later he would modestly suggest his success in the field of plant hunting was due to his being the first in the field. Over the years Henry sent a regular stream of thousands of specimens to Kew and then in 1888 was granted six months leave to gather plants. With his Chinese collectors, he gathered over 27,000 specimens in that one tour.

But then in 1889 he was forced to leave his beloved mainland China and work in the offshore island of Hainan. He hated it, hated the heat, the humidity, and to make matters worse, he succumbed to pernicious malaria. But during his convalescence he met and married Caroline Orridge in June 1891. Together they went to China and then Taiwan, but sadly she died in 1894.

Henry needed to keep his mind occupied and luckily received a new posting, to Mengzi (Mengtze) in Yunnan. He travelled there via the Red River in the very north of Vietnam, allowing him to botanise along the way. Mengzi was a blessing, a pleasant Mediterranean climate and a host of new plants to keep him busy.

Augustine Henry.

From a rhododendron viewpoint, he made his greatest discovery in this region. The very first sighting of *R. sinofalconeri* growing on the summit of Laojunshan near the Vietnamese border was perhaps the greatest thrill. This is the only known source of the plant in China, growing in a thicket on the summit of this isolated mountain at 8200–9500 ft (2500–2900 m). There are two known locations of *R. sinofalconeri* just across the border in Vietnam, but these were only discovered in the 1980s.

Over the next few years he was based at Mengzi or in Simao (Szemao) on the Laos border. And just as he had hoped, Kew sent a full-time collector to the region — Ernest Wilson and Augustine Henry met for the first time on 24 September 1899. Although there was nearly twenty years difference in age, the two men got along famously. Henry unstintingly gave Wilson all the information he could and even passed on his experienced plant collectors for him to employ. A year later, Augustine Henry left China for the last time, on 31 December 1900 — the end of an era. He had discovered over 1700 plants and sent home over 150,000 herbarium specimens. A phenomenal achievement.

PLANT COLLECTORS — FROM EARLY DAYS TO THE PRESENT

ERNEST WILSON 1876–1930

Ernest Wilson's path into plant hunting followed a fairly conventional route via the nursery trade and botanical gardens, including Kew. Then the famous Veitch Nurseries wanted someone to go to China and collect seeds of the *Davidia* tree located by Augustine Henry. Veitch persuaded him to travel via America where he spent some time at the Arnold Arboretum, a part of Harvard University in Boston. It was a lucky chance as Ernest Wilson became firm friends with the director of the gardens, Charles Sprague Sargent, and they agreed to keep in touch.

After three years in China, he came home to marry Ellen Ganderton (known as Nellie) in June 1902. Ever the one to worry about the future, he felt he had to consolidate his career and agreed to a second trip beginning in 1903, including a visit to the lush forest on the sacred mountain of Emeishan in Sichuan.

When the Veitch Nurseries folded, he needed a job and took some temporary work at the Kew herbarium. Although they only lived there a few months and subsequently lived in America for twenty years, Wilson always considered himself to be a Kewite and planned to retire there.

Charles Sargent reappeared on the scene to upset this domestic bliss, offering him the chance to collect in China for the Arnold Arboretum. Ernest was reluctant, he'd had enough of travel,

Ernest Wilson (below) was the first botanist to collect specimens of *R. watsonii* (right).

especially now he had a family, but the offer of 1500 pounds and a job at the Arnold Arboretum on his return was too good an offer to refuse. In a letter to Sargent he said, 'So you have captured me after all. Twelve months ago I would not have believed it possible for anyone to have persuaded me into revisiting China on any terms.'

Although the two men got on extremely well, from here on Wilson always seemed to be dancing to Sargent's tune. This time he had more leeway on what to collect, as there were no commercial parameters as when collecting for a profit-motivated nursery.

When Sargent died in 1927, Wilson succeeded him as director, but with Sargent gone, the funding decreased, adding to his stress levels. Having escaped the dangers of China, it was ironic that travel should take his life. On the 15 October 1930, he and his wife were killed in a car crash when their car spun off the road near Worcester, Massachusetts.

Without doubt the most successful plant collector of all time, he introduced more choice hardy plants than any before or since. He's credited with introducing over 1000 plants into cultivation but it's not just the sheer number but the garden-worthiness and hardiness of the plants he collected; he had a real eye for a garden gem. He was the first to collect two big-leaf species, namely *R. galactinum* and *R. watsonii*.

JOSEPH ROCK 1884–1962

Picture a little boy kneeling at a small altar in a humble dwelling in Vienna; on one side, his father is performing a religious ceremony and on the other his older sister Karolina is in silent prayer. This small boy is Joseph Rock and every day since the day she died when he was just six years old, they pray for his mother's soul. The children aren't allowed to play like others do; instead, they must constantly pay their respects to their mother's memory.

As you might imagine, young Joseph found it hard to make friends and eventually withdrew into his own private world. Frequently sick, he missed much of his schooling and took no interest even when he did attend. His day-to-day needs were taken care of by his sister but they were both totally dominated by their overly religious, depressive father. The one spark of originality from Joseph was when he took an interest in China and started to teach himself Chinese, at the age of thirteen.

From then on he was besotted with China, becoming reasonably proficient in Chinese and Arabic by his late teens. His natural ability with languages became the key to a unique and exciting life. In other ways he showed little interest in education and when his father told the lad to become a priest, he fled the country. But being poor he had to go on foot, and he walked and walked, travelling through Italy and on to north Africa, before working his passage to America in 1905. For a young man making his way in the world, what better place to aim for than the land of opportunity — the USA. There he drifted around until he got to Hawaii where his natural talent led to a teaching post at the university, but just when he seemed settled for the very first time, he was chosen to undertake a plant-hunting trip to India to try to find a cure for leprosy. He successfully accomplished this, which led to him taking up plant hunting full-time,

Joseph Rock's village in China (top) and Joseph Rock (bottom).

Francis Kingdon Ward and his wife Jean Macklin off plant hunting (below, top), and *R. magnificum*, one of the species first introduced by him (bottom).

eventually turning his sights to the riches of China. From 1922 till he was evicted in 1949 by the new Communist regime, he lived almost entirely in western China.

Despite a distinguished list of sponsors, including Harvard University, he suffered from lack of funds just like every other plant hunter. Mind you he did have more expensive tastes than most, travelling with a folding rubber bath, a collapsible bed, a wardrobe of stylish clothes, linen tablecloths and silver cutlery to serve his native Austrian dishes. He even carried a wind-up gramophone and opera recordings to while away the hours and impress the locals. He liked to impress, and when he met local dignitaries would dress up in his finery and be carried in on a sedan chair. 'You've got to make people believe you're someone of importance' was his justification.

Everything he did was meticulous; his specimens were immaculate. From a plant point of view it was unfortunate he rarely got to virgin ground untouched by Forrest or Ward. Rock was very keen on rhododendrons and sent back seed of many big-leaf species including *R. rex* which resulted in a very good seedling we now call *R. rex* 'Quartz'. He collected the first *R. rothschildii* and the red form of *R. arizelum*.

For his own amusement he studied the cultures and languages of the tribes of Yunnan, especially the Na-khi or Naxi people with whom he lived for many years. The house he lived in is still there and kept as a memorial. It is well worth a visit to get an insight into early plant hunting and the conditions the collectors endured. After the many years of risk and hardship he retired to Hawaii to work on his language and botany papers until his death from a heart attack in 1962.

Because of his childhood, he was never at ease in European society, but his interest in China led him into a new rewarding life. Joseph Rock certainly did his bit to make the world a better place. Lovers of rhododendrons, languages and geology all appreciate his efforts, but none more so than those with leprosy. What a wonderful achievement next to your name.

FRANK (FRANCIS) KINGDON WARD 1885–1958

Living in an era when to be English was to be superior to all other nationalities, Kingdon Ward enjoyed the role to the full. Always one for an adventure, he lived his life like a character in a novel. He was often arrogant, pompous and stubborn, but perhaps no more so than thousands of others who came through the English university system of the time.

Christened Francis Kingdon Ward, he continued to use his mother's maiden name of Kingdon to make himself sound more important. He's affectionately known as KW in plant circles because he collected over 20,000 seed lots, all properly catalogued and numbered with the prefix KW.

On the recommendation of Professor Balfour at Edinburgh Botanics, a friend of his father, he got an offer to gather alpine seeds in China. Arthur Bulley, owner of Bees Nursery, contracted him to collect alpine and herbaceous plants in north-west Yunnan, and he returned to Yunnan and Tibet for Bees in 1913. Bulley dithered about where to send him, but Kingdon Ward had already made up his own mind to return to the same area.

Late in the season, he took off on an unauthorised surveying expedition into Tibet and upset everyone in the process, especially the Chinese authorities who banned the locals from carrying his gear. Kingdon Ward liked Tibetans and the hill-tribe Lisu people, but not the Chinese, and so it seemed logical he should in future look to Tibet and Burma. Britain had only annexed northern Burma a year or two before in 1911, and this was one of the most remote outposts of the British Empire. Over the next few years he made numerous trips to Assam, Burma and Tibet. It seems glib to pass over them so quickly because he really did more travelling in these places than anyone else.

On his later trips he took his young second wife, Jean Macklin, and together they survived the great Assam earthquake of 1950 when trekking up the Brahmaputra River. Despite the horrors of their previous trip he couldn't stay away from the hills and they were back together in Burma in 1953 and again in 1956. Then on Easter Sunday 1958 they were having a drink in a pub in Kensington when he collapsed from a stroke and died.

Over the years he made a phenomenal twenty-one plant-hunting trips into Burma, Assam, south-west China, Tibet, Bhutan and Sikkim. His legacy to the world is a fantastic array of plants. Despite Arthur Bulley's initial doubts, the man obviously had an eye for a good garden plant. His life was terribly lonely at times, but in the last years of his life he had the genuine pleasure of being with Jean. Despite their age difference this was a real love match and they shared the triumphs and tribulations together.

Even today you will find plants in gardens with a KW number. This is especially true of rhododendrons which became his speciality. Many of the big-leaf rhododendrons were first introduced by him including the stately *R. magnificum*, *R. macabeanum* and *R. montroseanum*, as well as collecting numerous other big-leaf species. The beauty of this is we feel closer to the man who made such sacrifices to bring us new plants. What an astonishing life he led; what an incredible man.

TOM HUDSON, NEW ZEALAND

Tom was brought up in New Zealand living beside the famous Gwavas Garden in Central Hawke's Bay, managed by his father Michael Hudson. This would seem to be the perfect grounding for a plantsman, though Tom insists he was never very interested in plants as a youngster. He became a plant fanatic when he moved to Cornwall in England when the Cornish branch of the family ran out of heirs and Tom moved from New Zealand to take over the estate in Par, Cornwall.

As an explorer, he cut his teeth gathering seeds in Taiwan and then Bhutan, and subsequently South America. But it's southern China and particularly the western province of Yunnan where he's done most of his searching. Having said that, he's also discovered big-leaf rhododendrons in Vietnam.

Tom is the perfect travel companion if you're roughing it in the wilds. Never phased by events; always placid and cheery — the sort of man you'd hunt tigers with. Happy to trek with any like-minded soul, he's travelled with Edward Needham, Maurice Foster and most of the recent people listed here.

R. macabeanum (top) showing foliage and flower head and *R montroseanum* (bottom) in flower and with seed head.

Tom Hudson with *R suoilenhense* in North Vietnam.

At the end of a trip he distributes his seeds and field notes to avid plant enthusiasts, then continues with his quiet family life in deepest Cornwall. Don't expect to find him up on a podium showing slides to gardening groups or plant societies — it's not his scene. However, his garden is becoming a Mecca for serious 'plantaholics'. One only has to read John Grimshaw's book *New Trees*, sponsored by the International Dendrology Society, to realise how crucial Tom has been to reviving the plant-hunting scene. It seems every second plant in there was either discovered by or is grown by Tom in Cornwall. With his New Zealand background his collecting is much more diverse, knowing as he does that there's a climate somewhere to suit his new finds. He's willing therefore to collect palms, *Schefflera* and *Arisaema*, and semi-tropical plants of all descriptions.

KEITH RUSHFORTH, DEVON, ENGLAND

Keith is a tree man through and through, and makes his living as an arboriculturist. Added to this, he's also written a host of books on trees and shrubs, including tree guides for Britain and the USA. His articles appear in both regular gardener and more learned botanical magazines. Keith writes in an engaging manner and manages that tricky task of including technical information without losing the armchair reader.

Keith writes well, in fact he does everything well. He has an encyclopaedic knowledge even down to the collection number on his plants. His field notes are meticulous, and future generations will be thankful for his diligence.

Plant hunting is Keith's real passion and he's spent time trekking through forests and mountains in search of new plants in the northern hemisphere. He is often the pioneer in areas where no European has been for decades, if at all. Tibet, Bhutan, Vietnam, they're all familiar hunting grounds. When out in the wilds, all thoughts of civilisation and comfort go out the window and, in the passion of the moment, things like food and beds become of secondary importance and are often forgotten altogether.

Keith Rushforth with two Chinese botanists studying *Abies ziyuanensis*.

Keith was the person who realised *R. kesangiae* from Bhutan was a new species. How many times had this plant been seen since Griffith first collected it in 1838, but no one realised it was special. Then having beavered away researching the hidden places of Tibet for a likely region for exploration, he was rewarded with a new discovery of a brand new big-leaf rhododendron which he named *R. heatheriae* after his wife, in recognition of her tolerance of his long absences searching for plants.

Keith has collected seed of *R. suoilenhense*, *R. sinofalconeri* in Vietnam, *R. heatheriae* in Tibet and *R. kesangiae* in Bhutan. There is hardly a region where the big-leafs grow that is not familiar to him. Back at home, his passions include bamboo, alpacas, and his private arboreta in Devon in south-west England.

STEVE HOOTMAN, RHODODENDRON SPECIES BOTANICAL GARDEN, WASHINGTON STATE, USA

Steve is the curator and executive director of the Rhododendron Species Botanical Garden in Washington State, USA. But when he wears his other hat, he's off in the wilds of Nagaland or Arunachal Pradesh searching for rhododendrons. Acknowledged as a world expert on Ericaceae, and like so many 'plantaholics', he is also besotted with big-leaf rhododendrons. He's never happier than searching for them in the wild mountains.

But he is unusual in another way, too. Many plant fanatics are not great garden designers and only care about finding the right spot for a plant. Steve is a committed gardener and is keen to share his knowledge and improve the gardening experience of others. A large part of his role at the Species Garden is sharing information with members and gardeners, a role he relishes and enjoys.

In 2003, he discovered *R. macabeanum* growing at 12,500 ft (3800 m) on Mt Saramati in Nagaland, at a much higher altitude than previous collections. Hopefully these plants will be a

Steve Hootman, director of the Rhododendron Species Botanical Garden, USA (right) with Andrew Brooker, garden manager at Pukeiti Rhododendron Trust, New Zealand (left).

hardier version. Steve and his team were the first Europeans to scale Mt Saramati. On the same mountain, he made a significant discovery even if it was in the negative. Searching for the elusive *R. wattii*, which is known to grow on this mountainside, he did find the plants but came to the conclusion that it's a natural hybrid between *R. macabeanum* and *R. arboreum* with both plants being the only contenders for parentage.

Another notable discovery, in tandem with Ken Cox, was *R. kesangiae* growing in Arunachal Pradesh when it was thought to grow exclusively in Bhutan. And one of the collections from this trip may turn out to be a new population of the elusive *R. magnificum*, only discovered once in north Burma by Kingdon Ward. Our favoured giant rhododendrons are often hard to pin down and name, and often one needs to grow them in cultivation for a decade or more to discern their true identity. *R. falconeri* ssp. *eximium* was another surprise find in this region.

We look forward to more of his adventures, extending our knowledge of rhododendrons.

THE COX FAMILY, GLENDOICK GARDENS, PERTH, SCOTLAND

Whenever Kenneth Cox packs his bags and heads off plant hunting, he is following a long family tradition. His grandfather Euan Cox set the scene back in 1918 when he was invited to go plant hunting in north Burma by the very eccentric Reginald Farrer. It was to be Farrer's last trip; he died there in the cold wet hills aged just forty, leaving young Euan to make his own way home.

Cox was hooked and spent whatever time he could exploring for plants and so it was natural for his son Peter to follow in his footsteps, exploring Turkey, Nepal and China, always with the emphasis on rhododendrons.

Peter Cox set out to retrace many of the original collectors' key areas of discovery to try to reinforce what had been seen, collected, recorded or missed. One of the major challenges was getting into the old areas, which in many cases were now closed to outsiders, and took decades of negotiations to create openings. Between 1962 and 2002 he made eighteen trips to Asia, including Turkey, Northern India, Bhutan, Nepal, China-Yunnan, Sichuan, Guizhou and Tibet. He gradually involved his son Kenneth in the later trips as he reduced his time in the field, and Ken has now taken up the mantle along with many other younger collectors. One important key to all of this is the increased cooperation between plant collectors and the local botanical institutions so that many expeditions now work together to share knowledge and increase awareness of the fragility of the remaining flora and fauna.

While new species of plants have been discovered by Peter Cox, his lasting legacy will be the recollection and introduction of plants that have been lost or reduced to one or two specimens in cultivation and the observations made that enable botanists to sort out taxonomic problems.

Ken Cox, Peter's son, has taken exploration to a new level, accessing places previously thought impossible. Ken is never happier than when out exploring some hidden valley in Arunachal Pradesh or Tibet where few, if any Westerners have ever set foot. All three generations of Coxs have made some incredible plant discoveries, but it's hard to top Ken's recent triumphs: extending the known regions where certain species grow and the totally new species of big-leaf rhododendrons *R. heatheriae* in Arunachal Pradesh and *R. titapuriense* from southern Tibet.

All the Cox family seem to be multi-talented, creating exciting gardens, a thriving nursery business and as excellent authors of plant and plant-hunting books. They have made huge contributions to our knowledge of our favourite genus.

Peter (left) and Ken Cox at Glendoick, Perth, Scotland.

CHAPTER 4

Falconera subsection

Both the Falconera and Grandia subsections are very similar and some botanists think they should be merged. There are also some plants which don't fit easily or completely into one or the other of these subsections. Members of the Falconera subsection usually have thick woolly indumentum consisting of cup-shaped hairs as opposed to plastered indumentum in the Grandia subsection. Falconera subsection flowers have no nectar pouches unlike the Grandia subsection.

NOTE: Flowering times are given for the northern hemisphere, with southern hemisphere in brackets.

R. arizelum

(BALF.F. AND FORREST, 1920)
Pronounced aar-iz-eelum

R. arizelum in Yunnan (above), and growing at Pukeiti (opposite).

As a garden plant, this grows 10–25 ft (3–7.5 m) usually with a flat top, but in the wild it can reach up to 40 ft (12 m). The eight-lobed flowers are usually creamy-yellow with a maroon blotch. Depending on the clone, the flowers can be pale anaemic colours in shades of white, pink and yellow and they can also be purple or red. Often there is a crimson blotch at the base of the flower. The April to May flowers (August southern hemisphere) appear in a fairly tight round truss with about 15 to 25 oblique-campanulate flowers creating a dome as much as 5–6 in across (12.5–15 cm). Both calyx and ovary are densely tomentose and the 15–16 stamens are shorter than the corolla. Flowers April to May (Oct to Nov).

If you want to grow big-leaf rhododendrons, this species is a good place to start. It's hardier than most and is also very attractive. In fact, its cold-hardiness means it is more suited to colder regions such as Scotland. It is not so easy to grow in warmer climates such as New Zealand and Australia because it prefers colder, drier places.

R. arizelum was brought into cultivation by George Forrest in 1917, but it was most likely discovered by Jean Marie Delavay. Typically it grows in thickets and scrubland as well as conifer forests at an altitude of 8000–14,500 ft (2500–4500 m). It must be common because it was collected many times by Forrest, Farrer, Kingdon Ward and Rock in Yunnan, south-east Tibet and north Burma and, in more recent times, in Arunachal Pradesh. Of all the Chinese Falconera types, this is the one most directly linked to the Himalayan *R. falconeri*. It was once considered a form of *R. rex* to which it is closely allied.

In his book *Return to the Irrawaddy*, Frank Kingdon Ward described seeing hillsides of them at high altitude and said they were the last to flower, hinting this would make them suitable for colder climates, and goes on to describe them having 'deep foxy red woolly felt. Flowers pale yellow or less pleasantly a cold pinkish purple.'

There is also a form called *R. a.* var. *rubicosum* (now called Rubicosum Group), collected by Joseph Rock in 1923 on Mt Kenyichunpo in south-eastern Tibet in alpine meadows at 14,500 ft (4500 m). The flowers are ruby-red to crimson and thus the name *rubicosum* for red.

George Forrest found pure white forms in Yunnan and Burma but they don't seem to be in cultivation.

Above: *R. arizelum* Gongshan, Yunnan.

Opposite: *R. basilicum* at Benmore (top), and in the wild (bottom).

Award of Merit for foliage in 1963 for the clone called 'Brodick' from Brodick Castle Gardens, Isle of Arran, Scotland. It has strong purple-red flowers with a black throat, very nice indumentum beneath the leaf.

Hardiness rated at 3–4

Zones 7–9

The strongly veined dark green leaves often have a very prominent yellow midrib. The leaf shape varies from obovate to oblanceolate, 2.7–9 x 1–5 in (7–25 x 3–12 cm) and usually retained for several years. When they first emerge they are covered in grey indumentum on top but this peels away as the leaf expands. The shiny surface of the mature leaves is a distinctive feature, as are the club-like or obovate leaves which are wider at the end. The plant usually holds its leaves in a flat plane, making this one of the most decorative species. The bush itself is rounded in shape. Typically has red-brown peeling bark and often in shades of pink when young.

When the plant grows tall enough to turn the leaves, you will see the beautiful tan indumentum on the lower side of the leaf; it's very tactile, like velvet. The upper layer, too, is hairy with a coating of funnel-shaped hairs. It's pale pinkish-fawn when the leaf first unfurls and then mellows to cinnamon.

The young shoots are attractive as well, covered in a soft golden down. Forrest and Bayley Balfour called it *R. arizelum* meaning 'admirable, obvious or notable' because they thought it was a winner.

R. basilicum

(BALF.F. AND W.W.SMITH, 1916)
Pronounced baz-il-icum

R. basilicum is very easy to distinguish from other members of the Falconera subsection because the leaf petioles are flat and appear to have compressed wings. There are members of the Grandia such as *R. praestans* and *R. coryphaeum* (old name for *R. praestans*) with similar wings. You may wonder why it's not included in the Grandia subsection, but the thick woolly brown indumentum makes it a part of the Falconera subsection. These wings distinguish it from others in the subsection except *R. rothschildii* and *R. semnoides*.

The upper surface of the leaf is usually matt green but can be rich, shiny dark green. The undersurface is completely covered in thick woolly indumentum.

In cultivation it's a flat-topped tree with smooth peeling bark. It will grow in most sheltered gardens in the rhododendron regions of the world.

The flowers are usually creamy-white or yellow, sometimes with a hint of pink and a rich red crimson blotch in the centre. The initial pinky red quickly fades to off-white. The combination of new pink and older white flowers is appealing to some. There are muddy forms, so try to pick a good flowering clone. The flowers heads are held in a tight formation, making this a potentially superb flowering plant. Flowers March to May (August to September).

The Latin name means royal. It also has several synonyms, initially called *R. megaphyllum* by Balfour and Forrest, then named *R. regale* by Balfour and Kingdon Ward and is thought by some to be a southern form of *R. semnoides*.

Many trees labelled as *R. basilicum* in cultivation are most likely hybrids. Keith Rushforth rediscovered the true species on the Yongdeshan and recent collections south of the main Gaoligongshan on the Yunnan–Myanmar border region by him may offer new material or perhaps an entirely new species.

A very similar plant, called *R. grātum* by Chinese botanists, may also turn out to be new, or simply a form of *R. basilicum*. Several collections of *R. gratum* have been made from the Yunnan–Myanmar border.

First discovered by George Forrest in June 1913 in the region between the Shweli and Salween rivers in western Yunnan. Subsequently, it was found in other parts of north-west Yunnan and in northern Burma by Farrer, Kingdon Ward and Rock. Up to 30 ft (9 m) in the wild, it grows naturally on open rocky hillsides and in deciduous and conifer forests at 9–15,000 ft (2700–4500 m). In some ways it's a southern form of *R. arizelum* and they do seem similar.

Award of Merit 1956 from Minterne, Dorset, UK.

Hardiness rated at 3–4

Zones 8–9

FALCONERA SUBSECTION

R. coriaceum, north-west Yunnan (above), and growing at Olinda, Australia (below).

R. coriaceum

(FRANCH. 1898)
Pronounced corr-ee-ace-um

This is perhaps not the first choice when looking for big-leaf rhododendrons for your garden because the species is not the most dramatic or the best for flower display. Despite this, however, they have a certain charm about them and it's worth seeking out the good clones. Another adverse factor is that it is not as hardy as most other members of the subsection.

Usually a large shrub in cultivation noted for the long narrow leaves with a silver or grey underside. The indumentum completely covers the lower leaf. Later, these hairy leaves turn fawn or brown, while the upper surface is initially covered in white tomentum but later becomes olive-green. The young leaves are very attractive, covered in showy white hairs. Another appealing aspect is the tree remains fully clothed because the leaves stay on the bush for three to four years.

Large bell flowers are held in a loose truss, in shades of white or soft rosy pink with a crimson blotch in the middle. Some forms are pure white with a loose dangling truss. Around fifteen to twenty in a truss, these flowers appear in April to May (August to September). Most clones are free-flowering.

R. coriaceum is very similar to *R. rex* ssp. *fictolacteum* but has longer narrower leaves which are tapered at the base, while the leaves of *R. rex* are bigger. Both species have the distinctive white indumentum on the young leaves which is retained on the lower surface of the leaves in *R. coriaceum* and it also tends to have thin stems and branches as opposed to the stronger wood of *R. rex*. *R. galactinum* is closely allied as well.

The Latin name means leathery.

A clone called 'Morocco' from Windsor Great Park won an Award of Merit in 1953. It has white flowers with a crimson internal blotch.

Hardiness rated at 3–4

Zones 8–9

Originally found in north-west Yunnan by Abbé Soulié in 1895 and again a few years afterwards by Abbé Monbeig. Introduced by the indefatigable George Forrest in 1918. Found naturally in north-west Yunnan and south-east Tibet at 10,000–13,000 ft, (3000–4000 m). Grows 10–25 ft (3–8 m) in the wild.

The best garden clones are Forrest collections F 25622 and F 25872. They are prone to frost damage which can kill or distort flower and growth buds. Too much cold kills it outright.

R. decipiens

(LACAITA 1916)
Pronounced dey-sip-eans

A naturally occurring hybrid found in Sikkim and other regions. It's thought *R. hodgsonii* is the female parent and the male could be *R. falconeri* or *R. wightii*.

In the wild *R. falconeri* naturally hybridises with *R. hodgsonii* where the two species overlap. Naturally the early explorers thought they had found another species and described it as such but later it changed to *R.* x *decipiens*, meaning deceptive.

Peter Cox and his lifetime friend Peter Hutchison found hybrids between *R. falconeri* and *R. kesangiae* on the Takhti Peak in Bhutan in 1988.

The *R.* x *decipiens* plant itself is very handsome with rich felted new leaves covered in bronze and grey indumentum. When the leaves mature they have a matt finish, sometimes retaining the grey indumentum on top and always with a felty soft brown layer beneath. The terminal buds are pointy and the leaves big and bold.

Flowers are white or creamy-white and sometimes pink with a noticeable wine to purple blotch deep within.

R. falconeri at Crarae, Scotland.

R. falconeri ssp. falconeri

(HOOK. F. 1849)
Pronounced fal-con-eri

Typically a rounded tree reaching 10–50 ft (3–15 m), but they can be much bigger. Steve Hootman describes seeing 80-ft (24-m) trees near Barsey in Sikkim. This species is also found in Nepal, Bhutan and West Arunachal Pradesh growing on hillsides, sometimes in pure stands but more often found under the canopy of cool broad-leaf forest at altitudes of 8000–12,000 ft (2500–3600 m).

It was considered to be a magnificent find then and it still is today. If you can grow this in your garden then you are thrice blessed. Even a waist-high specimen is magical with enormous elliptic to obovate leaves as much as 1 ft (30 cm) long and 6 in (15 cm) wide, often with a scalloped edge. They are matt dark-green above with indented veins and, initially, the young leaves are covered with silvery hairs which rub off with time. On a good form, these leaves can compete with any rhododendron in the world.

R. falconeri growing at Crarae, Scotland, showing the attractive bark.

Lift the leaf and you will see it's covered in foxy-brown or rusty indumentum below. It's so lovely you'll find yourself 'turning over a new leaf' every time you walk by. As the tree matures and grows to eye level, the leaves are less inclined to be covered in indumentum on their upper surfaces, but the coating below becomes increasingly apparent and more handsome and ornamental as you look up at the rusty indumentum.

In a garden setting, this plant is so valuable it's worth finding a shady protected spot in a sheltered gully. Try to find a raised site where you will be able to look up at the leaves and appreciate the furry undersides of the fabulous leaves. Even the bark is attractive with peeling purple-brown trunks almost like an *Acer griseum* and this is best appreciated when the plant grows above you on a bank.

In spring, large dense heads of obliquely campanulate flowers appear in a racemose umbel. This is made up of fifteen to twenty-five waxy flowers in white or creamy-yellow, while some are more an opaque white. These magnificent heads can be fully 9 in (22 cm) across and are packed with twenty or so two-inch flowers. Some forms

R. falconeri ssp. *falconeri*, Pukeiti.

Although Joseph Hooker is usually credited with discovering this species in Sikkim in 1850, it seems likely that a Colonel Sykes was the first to send seeds to Britain in 1830. A notable and famous plant at the Glenarn garden in Scotland came from Hooker's first batch of seed.

R. falconeri was named by Joseph Hooker in honour of his friend Hugh Falconer (1808–1865), Superintendent of Saharanpur Gardens in Uttar Pradesh to the west of Nepal, and who later held the same post at Calcutta Botanic Garden. Like Hooker, Falconer was a fellow Scot and an all-round scientist who made a detailed study of Himalayan fossils. He was instrumental in setting up the tea and quinine industries in India. Hooker met him on his way to Sikkim.

The species was awarded an Award of Merit in 1922 when exhibited by Gill of Falmouth, and then given the prestigious AGM in 1984.

Hardiness rated at 3–4

Zones 8–9

have a large purple blotch in the base of the flower. The yellow forms are the more appealing, and some of the rich lemon-yellow varieties are heavenly. Each flower has eight to ten lobes with twelve to sixteen stamens, shorter than the tube.

What the individual flowers lack in size, they make up for with longevity as the waxy flowers can last for a month. The large globular heads of flower appear in the top of the tree in late April to May (October to November).

R. falconeri is the parent of some magnificent hybrids, notably *R.* 'Fortune', a cross made at Exbury gardens by Lionel de Rothschild. The full parentage is *R. falconeri* ssp. *falconeri* and *R. sinogrande* and it was rated a First Class Certificate (FCC) in 1938. The large flat-top heads of pale yellow flowers have a red inner blotch.

R. 'Muriel', a Loder cross between *R. falconeri* and *R. grande*, has magnificent leaves and crisp white flowers with a crimson blotch in the centre.

R. falconeri ssp. *falconeri* at Crarae, Scotland (top, left), at Pukeiti (bottom, left), and at Barsey, Sikkim (above).

Opposite: *R. falconeri* ssp. *eximium* in Ethel Joel Garden, Dunedin, New Zealand.

BIG-LEAF RHODODENDRONS

R. falconeri ssp. *eximium*

(NUTT. 1853) D.F. CHAMBERLAIN 1979
Pronounced ex-im-eum

R. falconeri ssp. *eximium* at Pukeiti.

The differences between this species and *R. falconeri* are now considered small and *R. eximium* was merged as a subspecies of *R. falconeri* in 1979. It differs in two main ways: the young leaves are covered in golden hairs, even on the upper surface, for the first year, whereas *R. falconeri* has hairless matt upper leaves when mature. *R. falconeri* is an upright tree whereas *R. eximium* is usually as wide as it is high and this seems fairly consistent regardless of where they grow naturally or where they are grown in cultivation. In the wild, *R. eximium* is often found in the same areas as *R. arizelum* and seems to have an affinity with it.

The young leaves on *R. falconeri* ssp. *eximium* are exquisite, with a rusty indumentum on the top surface and rich cinnamon beneath, standing out like no other large-leaf species and recognisable from a distance. Mature leaves are glorious paddles of foliage, matt-green above and rusty below; it's definitely one of the best rhododendrons for foliage. The trunks are exciting, too, being smooth-brown with peeling bark.

Initially, the flowers of *R. falconeri* ssp. *eximium* are a rose colour. They open to pink and then the older flowers at the base fade to creamy-white, while the top of the truss is still pink. At their best, they are just sublime. The flower head is a racemose umbel of twelve to twenty, obliquely campanulate flowers held together in a huge dense truss. Most versions are dense and compact but some forms can be open and lax. Stamens number ten to fourteen, all shorter than the flower tube and the ovary is densely glandular, not hairy. Flowers March to May (August to September). It's not the most hardy of species so a warm, sheltered site should be found.

The plant is much smaller in the wild than the potentially huge *R. falconeri* ssp. *falconeri*. Even the leaf size is smaller.

In Bhutan the *R. falconeri* ssp. *falconeri* are found in the west of the country and as you move to the east, you encounter mixed forms, like hybrids between the two, and then the real *R. falconeri* ssp. *eximium* in the east. It's as if the two merge in the middle. Confusing the issue even more is the fact that *R. falconeri* ssp. *falconeri* hybridises with the *R. hodgsonii* and with the Grandia subsection *R. kesangiae* in the middle part of Bhutan.

The same is true of *Pinus wallichiana* found in the west of Bhutan, with its short grey-blue needles. As you travel east, the pine needles get longer and by the time you arrive in the eastern part of Bhutan you find mostly long-needle *Pinus bhutanica*, which has only recently been accepted as a separate species. Those found in the extreme west and east are obviously different, but with both pines and rhododendrons found in the middle regions, it's more difficult to determine what they are.

The Latin name means excellent.

Award of Merit 1973 as a foliage plant, Royal Botanic Garden, Wakehurst Place.

Hardiness rated at 2–3

Zone 9

R. falconeri ssp. *eximium* at Pukeiti.

R. falconeri ssp. *eximium* at Gwavas Garden, New Zealand.

Possibly the first of the big-leaf rhododendrons to be discovered back in the early 1850s by Englishman Thomas Booth on the Oola mountains in Bhutan. Booth is one of the forgotten heroes, an amateur who wandered off into the Himalayas searching for plants. Nowadays he's chiefly remembered as the nephew of Thomas Nuttall, the English botanist who dominated American botany in the early 1800s, traversing virtually every state. Booth described this rhododendron as 'growing amidst ice and snow' up to 30 ft (9 m) high, growing on rocky slopes at 9000–11,000 ft (2700–3300 m). More recent collections have extended the known boundaries to include Arunachal Pradesh in north-east India, and some exciting-looking foliage plants with superb dark indumentum are now being grown from these sources.

A fairly recent form discovered by Peter Cox and Peter Hutchinson (C&H 427) has very pretty pink flowers and is worth seeking out. It may be hardier, too, because it was found in a pure stand on an exposed ridge. Thanks to Kenneth Cox and Steve Hootman, we now know this species extends beyond eastern Bhutan as they found it growing in Arunachal Pradesh at around 10,500 ft (3200 m). These are welcome additions to our gardens with their rosy-pink flowers and cinnamon-felted leaves.

FALCONERA SUBSECTION

R. galactinum at Benmore, Ernest Wilson collection.

> First collected by the ever industrious Ernest Wilson back in 1908 when he gathered seed capsules in west Sichuan. His collection number was Wilson 4254. The species wasn't even described until 1926 by Scottish botanist Harry Tagg based at Edinburgh Botanic Garden. In fact it is the most easterly of the Falconera subsection. Wilson said it was rare, and so it's proved to be as no other collector found it again until the late 1980s when Peter Cox and Peter Hutchison found it on several mountains in Sichuan, proving beyond doubt this is a recognised species and not a hybrid as some surmised.

R. galactinum

(BALF.F. 1926)

Pronounced galact-in-um

It's tempting to think the Latin name is somehow connected with distant galaxies but it's much more boring, referring to the Greek word *gala* for milky, from the white flowers.

The plant has short stubby foliage buds covered in indumentum rather than the more typical pointed buds of the other members of the subsection. More observant folk might notice the glabrous ovary, the only one in the subsection. All other Falconera have masses of tomentum on the ovary. The leaves can be up to 8 in (20 cm) long and 4 in (10 cm) wide. They are quite dull on top with a thick pelt of brown indumentum covering the whole undersurface.

It's not one of the exciting species grown for spectacular leaves; it's more of a collector's item. Neither is it common in cultivation, having come initially from one source, but, in time, new forms will become available as it was collected in Sichuan in the 1980s by American collector Warren Berg. Some of these new clones are growing well in the Rhododendron Species Foundation Garden in Seattle.

But while the leaves may not be the most exciting, the flowers are truly beautiful. They are a pure white with a rich wine blotch within. As the flower matures, this wine blotch often bleeds into the flower creating a pinky-purple hue which is nevertheless very attractive. On the plus side the plant is much hardier than most big-leafs.

Typically the thin white flowers have a small deep rich-red blotch within. Some clones tend more to pink, but white is the most common form. Flowers April to May (September). The combination of small dainty flowers and relatively small leaves makes this look more like a typical rhododendron.

Hardiness rated at 4

Zones 7–9

R. heatheriae
(K. RUSHFORTH 1999)

New to the fold, this recently discovered species has great potential. First discovered by Keith Rushforth in south-east Tibet on the west side of Showa-La at 13,500 ft (4150 m), and just a little north of the dip in the border at the northern boundary of Arunachal Pradesh. This is on the famous Brahmaputra River Frank Kingdon Ward was always so keen to explore, and he eventually realised his dream in the 1950s. The river canyon allows moist, warm air from India to flow this way, encouraging rich verdant forest. The Chinese plan to build hotels and tourist infrastructure nearby to show off their equivalent of the Grand Canyon.

I asked Keith about the trip. 'The party members on that trip were Peta and Vinh Burton Smith, Patrick Forde and David Lang — first trip David had made with me since the 1985 Bhutan one, although we had met at Sinclairs at Bagdogra as he was exiting from his first trip to Sikkim at the same time. Peta brought me a specimen the first evening we arrived at the yak hut on the far side of the Showa-La. I immediately concluded it was new. David Chamberlain concurred when I showed him specimens.'

R. heatheriae showing dead flowers and seed heads (above) and indumentum (below).

Keith rather touchingly named this new species after his wife Heather as an acknowledgement of her support for his work and his frequent absences from home in the pursuit of plants. The irony is the plant is too tender to grow in his Devon garden but it does survive in Cornwall, Scotland and Northern Ireland in sheltered warm gardens, and it does well in the Pacific north-west, in the Seattle area.

Since Keith's initial discovery, somewhat similar plants have been found in Arunachal Pradesh directly south of Keith's location and midway north to south in this remote country. Here, near Singa on the Abroka Pass, these plants were also discovered by Tom Hudson, Steve Hootman and Ken Cox. This form, however, has much larger leaves that are broader but with the same general shape and appearance, but with longer petioles and much paler indumentum.

Keith's original version has copper undersides and the leaves have a very short, winged petiole. The blooms are not known. The strong fimbriated cup-shape hairs make it a part of the Falconera subsection. Keith describes it as a 16.5-ft (5-m) tree, occasionally growing to 26 ft (8 m) with flaky bark as fine as any splendid *R. falconeri*. Leaves are cuneate, obovate, maximum 12 x 4 in (30 x 10 cm) but mainly less than 8 x 2–3 in (20 x 5–7 cm). They are rounded mucronate to faintly emarginate at the apex, with the base of the leaf decurrent on the short, winged petiole; underside densely fulvous, hairy as in *R. arizelum*. Ovary rufous, hairy, 0.4–1 in (1–2.5 cm).

R. hodgsonii

(HOOK. F. 1851)
Pronounced hodg-son-i

First discovered in Bhutan in 1838 by William Griffith, though Joseph Hooker gets the credit after he found it in 1849 and named it after his good friend and mentor Brian Hodgson. An old hand by the time Hooker reached India, Hodgson was retired from the East India Company and living in Darjeeling. He hosted Hooker for long periods and gave him lots of useful advice and encouragement.

A bit like the man it's named after, this is a character plant rather than a beautiful one. It does have a certain rugged charm but it lacks the elegance of others in the Falconera subsection. In cultivation, they tend to be short chunky plants with a flat top. Even the leaves and flowers are not as beautiful as others in the subsection. Having said that, there are superb forms about and it's worth seeking out the best ones.

Leaves are obovate to elliptic, grey, rough and leathery with a tactile layer of rich brown indumentum beneath. These leaves are anything from 6–12 in (15–30 cm) long and up to 5 in (13 cm) wide but they tend to be on the smallish side. They're usually shiny above but can have a thin layer of tomentum, giving a ghostly grey cast. The conical growth buds are very distinctive and usually covered in greyish tomentum.

Depending on the clone, the flowers can be anything from pink to lilac, purple to red. Some clones are very good but others are rather dowdy in colour. Whatever the colour, it seems to fade quite quickly, so perhaps it's not the best species to grow for flowering display.

R. hodgsonii, Yumthang Valley, Sikkim.

BIG-LEAF RHODODENDRONS

A natural hybrid between two Bhutanese species — R. hodgsonii x R. kesangiae.

Flower trusses are a flat-topped racemose umbel of twelve to twenty-five tubular campanulate flowers, with seven or eight lobes and appear any time from March through to May (August to September). Some forms are scented.

In the wild, *R. hodgsonii* is a rounded spreading shrub or small tree usually growing to about 20 ft (6 m) but has been known to grow up to 40 ft (12 m). The bark is usually smooth and shiny and can be a very attractive feature, ranging from pale shades through to hot red or orange which shows up from a distance. Found in mixed forest and coniferous *Abies* forest 9500–14,000 ft (3000–4300 m) in Nepal, Sikkim and Bhutan through to Assam and south Tibet. In recent times it's been found in western Arunachal Pradesh by Kenneth Cox and Steve Hootman under the number KCSH 0367. It sometimes grows in the open on high ridges, and it has been known to hybridise in the wild with *R. falconeri*.

Award of Merit 1964 for a clone 'Poet's Lawn' exhibited by Windsor Great Park, London.

Another fine clone is 'Harp Wood'.

Hardiness rated at 4

Zones 8–9

R. hodgsonii at Glendoick, Scotland.

FALCONERA SUBSECTION

R. mechukae

(A.A. MAO & A. PAUL, 2013)
Pronounced mech-u-ky and named after the valley it grows in.

This is a brand new species discovered in the Mechukha Valley, West Siang, Arunachal Pradesh, north-east India in 2011. Flowering from February to March (July to August) the bright pink flowers stand out in the mainly old *Abies*, *Taxus* and *Pinus* evergreen forest at an elevation around 7850 ft (2400 m).

It is a shrub or small tree 16–32 ft (5–10 m) tall with rough, peeling, brown bark. Leaves are long and elliptic in shape with two layers of indumentum below; the bottom layer compact, and the upper one made up of dense rust-coloured, cup-shaped hairs. These cup-shaped hairs put it into the subsection Falconera. The petioles are 1–2 in (3–5 cm) long and covered with rufous indumentum.

The large flower trusses are twelve to eighteen tubular-campanulate bells, rich pink to magenta purple with a dark reddish blotch in the base, and eight-lobed with wavy margins. Flowering so early in the year is a bonus for the enthusiast but if and when it reaches cultivation, both the flowers and new growth might prove susceptible to frost damage.

This species is ranked as critically endangered because it has only been found in the one area, about 3.8 sq miles (10 sq km) in extent, and is subject to local pressure for timber extraction and firewood gathering. Seedling regeneration, while reasonable, is subject to very dry and cold winter conditions resulting in much loss of young plants. Given the overall situation it is easy to see why the Indian botanists think the species could be extinct sooner rather than later if measures are not put in to place to prevent more forest depletion. Further study is needed to ascertain what might be done to save this species, whether in situ, which is desirable, or ex-situ, from seed obtained from the population and shared among growers who are keen to keep the gene pool alive. Let's hope something can be done before another 'Dodo' event.

Above and right: *R. mechukae*.

Latin name means distinguished.

Hardiness rated at 3–4

Zone 9

R. preptum

(BALF.F., FORREST 1919)
Pronounced prept-um

This is not a common plant in cultivation because it's not often found in the wild. In fact, some botanists query whether it is a true species as it has only been collected three times, each time by George Forrest. First discovered in Burma in May 1919 and subsequently in another part of Burma and then north-west Yunnan. It's found at 11,000–12,000 ft (3300–3700 m) in mixed scrub and bamboo thickets.

The leaves are matt green on top and covered in indumentum below. The flowers are quite pretty in a creamy-white or perhaps with a hint of pink.

Some suggest it's a naturally occurring wild hybrid of *R. arizelum*, *R. coriaceum* or *R. fictolacteum*.

R. rex ssp. *fictolacteum* flowering profusely, Cangshan, Dali, western Yunnan.

FALCONERA SUBSECTION

R. rex ssp. fictolacteum

(BALF.F. 1886) D.F.CHAMBERLAIN 1979
Pronounced ficto-lact-ee-um

Now regarded as a subspecies of *R. rex*, this is a worthy addition to any garden, due in part to its hardiness and robust nature. It's been in cultivation a long time and so there are some big specimens growing in well-established gardens. It is the most common of the big-leafs in China and therefore the most common in cultivation.

This species grows in open country as well as in mixed and conifer forest at elevations of 10,000–14,500 ft (3000–4500 m). Joseph Rock said it formed almost pure rhododendron forest in open alpine regions at 14,000 ft (4200 m) in south-east Tibet. Kingdon Ward, also, found stands of it at 10,000 ft (3000 m) in western China, and sent seeds home. He describes them as 40–50 ft (12–15 m) high and as having 'immense leaves' and yet many forms in cultivation are much smaller.

Above and below: *R. rex* ssp. *fictolacteum*, on the Cangshan, Yunnan.

Latin name means false lacteum which in turn means milky.

Award of Merit for foliage, 1923.

A good clone named 'Cherry Tip' from Minterne, Dorset, UK received an Award of Merit in 1953. The flowers are cherry-pink opening to white with a hint of pink. Received the prestigious AGM in 1984.

Hardiness rated at 3

Zone 9

This probably accounts for its hardiness and the ability to grow in open alpine territory. For gardeners starting a collection of giant rhododendrons, this is a good species to begin with because it's tough and tolerates more cold than most. Another advantage is the plant is inclined to bloom early in its life.

The leaves are smooth and shiny dark green above with a continuous thick dense russet or brown indumentum beneath. It's one of the best for that rich foxy pelt we all so admire.

Flowers appear April to May (August to September) and are usually white or creamy-white with a pale pink frill around the corolla. The inside is decorated with pink or purple spots and often has a crimson blotch. There are definite similarities with *R. rex* spp. *rex* but the flowers are usually paler and smaller, and the leaves are smaller, too, with dark indumentum.

R. rex ssp. *fictolacteum* is frequently found in the wild in west and north-west Yunnan and south-east Tibet, while Kingdon Ward and others found it in upper Burma.

But the plant was first discovered by Jean Marie Delavay in May 1886 in the Cangshan near Dali, western Yunnan, at around 10,500 ft (3200 m). Mostly Delavay collected only herbarium specimens, but on this occasion he was so enamoured by the enormous leaves he sent seed to the botanist Adrien René Franchet, in Paris, and he in turn gave seedlings to Kew in 1889. Franchet was so overwhelmed by the sheer volume of specimens he received from Delavay, over 200,000 in all, that much of what he collected never saw the light of day.

R. rex ssp. rex
(H.LÉVEILLÉ 1914)

In the wild, the tree reaches 40 ft (12 m) but you'll be lucky to have one half that height in cultivation. An upright tree with robust chunky stems, and the young wood covered in whitish indumentum.

Leaves vary and can be dull matt green through to extremely attractive deep green above, while some forms have rich dark shiny leaves. Not always the most exciting leaves, but what they lack in ornamentation they make up for in size as they can be up to 18 in (45 cm) long. The undersurface is more showy, covered in greyish-brown indumentum.

The flowers are usually rose-coloured often with a dark basal blotch and spotting within, but they can also be white or creamy-white. It has between twenty and thirty flowers in a head. Flowering time is April to May (August to September).

R. rex ssp. rex is considered to be one of the more cold-hardy of the large-leaf species, alongside R. rex ssp. fictolacteum, R. watsonii and R. galactinum. This makes it the ideal beginner plant of the subsection. It's very similar to R. rex ssp. fictolacteum, but the leaves are usually much bigger and bolder. Indumentum beneath the leaves is usually paler. The flowers, too, are much bigger. Kingdon Ward was especially proud of his R. rex KW 4509 found at 10,000 ft (3000 m) in western China. This beautiful clone has white flowers and a central crimson blotch.

R. rex ssp. rex at Meerkerk (above) and *R. rex ssp. rex* 'Quartz' (below) at Pukeiti.

Rex in Latin means king.

First Class Certificate for foliage exhibited as *R. fictolacteum* in 1935. It was the KW 4509 clone.

Award of Merit, 1946 for KW 4509 clone.

Award of Merit, 1955 for the clone 'Quartz' collected by Rock, R 03800 which is white, tinged pink

Hardiness rated at 4

Zones 7–9

Discovered on Mt Lo-Shan in north-east Yunnan in 1911 by Edouard-Ernest Maire (1848–1932) a French collector best remembered for *Mahonia mairei* with rich yellow, sometimes orange, flowers. Subsequently, this rhododendron was found by other collectors in north-west Yunnan and south-west Sichuan at around 10,000–14,000 ft (3000–4300 m). It's apparently very common in the wild and even forms pure stands in places. George Forrest was the first to introduce it in 1913, seed batch F 10974, collected in north-east Yunnan.

First collected by Joseph Rock in 1929 under number R 157, but then he came across it again in 1948 in north-west Yunnan, growing in fir forest at 12,800 ft (4000 m).

Poor old Rock does not have many firsts because he was collecting in western China many years after Delavay, Forrest and Kingdon Ward. Even in this instance, he never knew it was a first because the plant was not properly classified until 1972, ten years after his death in 1962.

If you want to find some in the wild, the only known location is the Ta Pao Shan between Weixi and the Mekong River in west Yunnan, growing in mixed forest at 11,000–13,000 ft (3300–4000 m).

Hardiness rated at 3–4

Zones 8–9

R. rothschildii at Glendoick, Scotland (top) and in flower at Benmore, Scotland (right).

R. rothschildii

(H.H. DAVIDIAN 1972)
Pronounced Rothschild-ee-i

Named after Lionel de Rothschild (1882–1942), the man who established the Exbury gardens in Hampshire, England, and whose abiding passion was rhododendrons. It's not very common in cultivation but it is a good doer, a sturdy and hardy plant growing to 10 ft (3 m) in cultivation and twice that height in the wild.

The leaves taper at the base and the petiole is winged or compressed. These huge paddle leaves can be 14 in (36 cm) long, sometimes with a shiny top surface, sometimes a matt finish. There is usually a thin spotty layer of rufous indumentum underneath. The easy way to distinguish it from the closely related *R. basilicum* is this indumentum.

The flower buds begin almost crimson and then open to creamy-white, sometimes with a hint of yellow. Each flower has a rich crimson blotch within. Flowers appear in April to May (August to September).

Some botanists regard this as a naturally occurring hybrid of perhaps *R. arizelum* or *R. praestans*.

R. semnoides

(TAGG, FORREST 1926)
Pronounced sem-noy-dees

Not terribly well known and some botanists says it's a northerly form of *R. basilicum*, while others suggest it could be a naturally occurring hybrid.

In cultivation it grows to 10 ft (3 m) and can be double that in the wild. The foliage varies, but is usually rich dark green and shiny on the upper surface; underneath is a complete layer of fawn-brown indumentum. Definitely worth growing for the foliage alone and because it's also quite tough and reasonably hardy.

The bell flowers can be white or creamy-white, or often white suffused with pink, and each one with a typical red blotch inside. With regular frilly-edged flowers, they can be quite appealing. Flowers appear in April to May (August to September).

The Latin name is a bit obscure. It means resembling semnum (praestans).

Hardiness rated at 3–4

Zones 8–9

This plant hails from north-west Yunnan and south-east Tibet, growing at 12,000–13,000 ft (3600–4000 m). It was discovered in Tibet by George Forrest in 1922, but despite being in cultivation for nearly 100 years it is still a disputed species. In more recent times Steve Hootman and Tom Hudson found a few specimens growing among a colony of *R. praestans* in the very north-west part of Yunnan. *R. arizelum* was also discovered in the same locale, growing higher up the slopes.

R. semnoides showing its distinctive foliage: growing at Glendoick, Scotland (left), and this rare species showing underside of the leaf in the wild (below).

For a long time this plant was only known from one source. It was collected by Augustine Henry about 1898 in south-east Yunnan close to the Vietnam border and near where he was stationed as a customs officer. The name is very appropriate because the plant looks very much like *R. falconeri* which grows way over to the west in the Himalayas. This being the Chinese version, it's called *sinofalconeri*, sino being China. The way to separate the two species is the lack of any pitting on the lower leaf surface of *R. sinofalconeri*.

Tom Hudson, from Tregrehan in Cornwall, was probably the first Westerner to see this species growing in Vietnam and he tells me *R. sinofalconeri* only occurs around the Sapa area on Fansipan mountain south of the Red River with *Abies fansipanensis* and bamboo scrub. As he says, the plant also grows in south Yunnan on the north side of the Red River, mostly around 9000 ft (2700 m). There are small morphological foliar differences, but the flowers both fit the species type. The biggest plants he's seen are around 30 ft (9 m).

In recent times Westerners have found more colonies of the species growing in Vietnam in regions previously off limits. Typically found around 9,000–10,000 ft (2700–3000 m) but can be found at 5000 ft (1500 m) on up. In the wild, the plant grows around 20 ft (6 m) high.

Since the initial Vietnam find, Peter Cox and Steve Hootman found more colonies in southern Yunnan in 1995. These two colonies, separated by a national border, are very different in appearance to the naked eye but match up under the microscope. The plants Peter Cox and Steve Hootman discovered in 1995 are not far away on a small peak called Laojunshan near Wenshan and relatively close to Augustine Henry's original population in Pingbian county in the Daweishan Range. The plants were found near the summit, from 8000–9500 ft (2500–2900 m). This place is approximately 37 miles (60 km) from the Vietnam border and 60–93 miles (100–150 km) away from Fansipan mountain.

R. sinofalconeri on the Laojunshan, south Yunnan border with Vietnam (above left and right).

R. sinofalconeri
(BALF.F. 1916)
Pronounced sino-fal-con-eri

The Chinese version found north of the Red River is blessed with a rounded leaf and loose, pale indumentum, while the Vietnam form found south of the Red River has a more pointy elliptic-shaped leaf with tight, darker coloured indumentum.

The developing growth buds of the Vietnam form are very pointy. When the new leaves emerge, the stem is encased in attractive red bracts and there is a thin covering of whitish indumentum on the upper surface. Both fall off as the leaves mature. The outer edges of the leaves are sometimes wavy.

The flowers come in various shades of yellow and can be anything from rich yellow to pale lemon-yellow to cream. Whichever it is, you will want one for your garden. It's one of the better big-leafs for flower colour. Flowers appear in April to May (August to September).

Because of recent excitement over what is effectively a new species, *R. sinofalconeri* is finding its way into major collections.

Hardiness rated at 2–3, but being relatively new we're still discovering what it's capable of; so far it's proving to be much hardier than first thought. This fits in with many plants discovered in north Vietnam, which were originally thought to be tender simply because of the latitude and the tropical nature of most of Vietnam. We're discovering many plants found in the northern mountains are hardier than some Himalayan forms of the same thing. *R. nuttallii* would be an example. Apart from the mountainous homeland, the other feature that suggests hardiness is the cold air which sweeps south during winter.

Zones 8–9, and it could be much lower

R. titapuriense

(A.A. MAO, K.N. E. COX & D.F.CHAMBERLAIN., SP. NOV.2011)

In 2000, Ken Cox discovered a new species which rivals George Forrest's 80 ft (24 m) *R. protistum (giganteum)*. In the Pemako region of Arunachal Pradesh, Kenneth found a grove of tree rhododendrons which may be as high as 100 ft (30 m). It seems 90 ft (27.5 m) is confirmed, but it's hard to measure trees in this dense forest on such steep slopes.

In 2005, Ken Cox, along with Tom Hudson and Steve Hootman, found more of these in a new location, but the same general region, so it's reassuring to think there is more than one population. Steve describes the trees and the situation:

> 'In 2005, we found another population of this species and were amazed at its mammoth proportions. In a deep ravine, at around 8000 ft (2438 m), stood a widely scattered grove of several gigantic trees of this extraordinary species. The largest specimens were easily over 80 ft (24 m) and likely over 100 ft (30 m) in height and several feet in diameter, rivalling, if not surpassing, the massive trees of R. protistum (giganteum) that I, and many others, have observed in the primeval forests along the Salween River in western Yunnan. These ancient specimens of R. protistum were first found by George Forrest and have long been considered the largest rhododendrons in the world.

> 'Of course, since all of the foliage was high up in the canopy of our mammoth species nova, we were able to get a proper look at only a few small specimens of this new forest giant. It has large but not massive leaves, with a thick reddish-brown indumentum on the lower surface, which is, to my eye's casual observation, reminiscent of the indumentum on R. mallotum a member of subsection Neriiflora. Under the microscope, however, the indumentum of this new species was composed of strongly cup-shaped hairs, placing it in subsection Falconera. This should prove to be an exciting new garden plant for gardens in very mild climates.'

What sheltered valleys and dense forest to hide such monsters for so long. The location was the Upper Siang area of Arunachal Pradesh, north-east India, in the middle of the province but up on the northern border of Tibet at around 8000 ft (2400 m). It's a sacred Buddhist locality, thought to be the centre of the earth or earth mother. The immediate region where the plant was found is Titapuri, part of the Titapuri, Pemshri and Riutala mountain complex, and thus the species name.

R. titapuriense growing in the wild (top) and leaf detail (bottom).

This new member of the Falconera subsection has dense foxy-brown indumentum and cup-shaped hairs. Young leaves have indumentum on the top surface as well. Few flowers have been seen but some creamy-white ones have been spotted. As it was discovered at a fairly low altitude, below *R. heatheriae*, it is unlikely to be very hardy. It also reportedly comes into growth very early in spring, increasing the risk of frost damage, but small plants have survived their first winter in Cornwall, coping with minus 7°C.

R. species nova

Steve Hootman says that in the remote and poorly explored mountains of the Pemako region in Arunachal Pradesh, north-eastern India, there are other new species and on another expedition there two, probably new, species of big-leaf rhododendrons were found. One of these was at around 9200 ft (2800 m) where it occurred in mixed temperate forest. As noted by Peter Cox, it formed a tree to 40 ft (12 m) and had peeling bark and large leaves. These had a thin but continuous rufous indumentum beneath and the buds looked similar to those of *R. protistum*, whereas the capsules looked somewhat like those of *R. arizelum* but were much stouter. In general appearance, the *species nova* appeared to Peter to be closest to *R. sinofalconeri*. The second species was labelled as *R. grande* affinity and was found over a wide altitudinal range centring on an elevation of around 9500 ft (2900 m). It occurred in mixed forest and in *Abies* (true fir) forest and also grew to about 40 ft (12 m) in height. The leaves were silvery, sometimes buff, beneath with buds similar to those of *R. hodgsonii* but markedly smaller, and ranging from black to green in colour. According to Peter Cox's field notes, it was quite common.

> Plant hunting in Arunachal Pradesh has opened up new avenues and new forms of big-leaf rhododendrons. Keith Rushforth says, 'The area from Tongri to Poshing La seems to represent a melting pot with elements of *R. grande, R. kesangiae, R. pudorosum, R. magnificum, R. sinogrande* and *R. montroseanum* types or relatives occurring together.'
>
> Of course, it will take years to fully evaluate the garden-worthiness of each of these new introductions. They are representatives, or perhaps proof, of the seemingly never-ending diversity of the genus *Rhododendron*. Who knows what other new rhododendron treasures await 'discovery' in the still unexplored reaches of the Sino-Himalaya? With each new exploratory expedition, our knowledge of this remarkable genus is enhanced and expanded. We can only hope that at least a portion of the forests in which these elegant and beautiful plants occur will be preserved.

In addition, there is another new species that Ken Cox and Steve Hootman first saw in 2003 in Arunachal Pradesh. At the time it was referred to as *R. magnificum* aff. They saw it again in 2005 near the *R. titapuriense* population. Subsequently, Keith Rushforth, Alan Clark and others then followed in their tracks and into nearby locations and collected this same taxon. This is definitely a new species first introduced under the 2005 collection, number APA#035.

The *species nova* HECC#10010 subsection Falconera from Arunachal Pradesh is another exciting new prospect and is being sold by the Coxes and by the Rhododendron Species Botanical Garden (RSBG) in Seattle. This is a new species to science, recently collected by Peter and Kenneth Cox for the first time at 7400 ft (2200 m) in a previously unexplored part of the eastern Himalaya. From Peter's field notes he states it is 'large-leaved, nearest *R.sinofalconeri*?' It does not quite match anything seen before, and, if truly near *R. sinofalconeri* taxonomically, it is a most amazing discovery. It has very distinct foliage and quite early into new growth, requiring protection from early spring frosts.

Opposite: *R. titapuriense* — flower detail.

CHAPTER 5

Grandia subsection

The plants in the Falconera and Grandia subsections are very similar and there are some which don't fit easily or completely into one or the other. Some botanists think they should be merged.

Plants in the Grandia subsection, however, usually have thin, plastered indumentum rather than the rich lush felted layers we see in the *R. falconeri* types. And the flowers of many in the Grandia subsection have nectar pouches in the base of the tube, unlike those in the Falconera subsection where they don't. Grandia types are more prone to heat stress and damage from strong sunlight as well as being more tender to cold and frosts.

Note: Flowering times are given for the northern hemisphere, with southern hemisphere in brackets.

R. grande
(WIGHT, 1847)
Pronounced gran-dee

Although this species was the basis for the Grandia subsection, it is not the most spectacular or beautiful. For all that, it is still a handsome species that most people would be proud to have in their garden. With oblong to oblong-lanceolate leaves 5–15 in (12–38 cm) long and 3–6 in wide (7–15 cm), it is still rather special. The new young growth and branchlets are covered in white tomentum, while the mature leaves are usually dull green on the surface and have a shiny silvery indumentum beneath. The new growth is particularly attractive, appearing as silvery-white or purple-bronze spears above the old darker green leaves.

Opposite: *R. grande* at Pukeiti.

R. grande at Pukeiti.

The oblique campanulate flowers appear very early in the season and this can be a problem in cold regions, if it chooses to flower in February or March (July or August). Frost damage is almost inevitable for much of the temperate world in this season. The flowers initially come from pink buds and open to pure or creamy-white with purple blotches within, with eight purple nectar pouches. These trusses can be up to 7 in (18 cm) wide with around fifteen to twenty-five eight-lobed flowers in a loose arrangement. The ovary is tomentose, and the sixteen to eighteen stamens are shorter than the corolla. There are forms around with hints of yellow, or even pink, flowers, but they can also be a dirty off-white, so it pays to pick a good clone. Flowers on some forms are scented. Unfortunately, as with all large-leaf species, they take many years to flower from seed and few clones are available for specific selection.

Flowering from February onwards, there is always the risk of cold and frost damage to the flowers. Ideally the plant needs a mild climate so the flowers can open without damage, and like so many of the big-leafs, it needs a good site in a sheltered garden with sufficient moisture throughout the year. The attractive, often bronze-red early growth can be damaged or killed by frosts. Plants are prone to wind damage as well. In the wild the tree can reach 50 ft (15 m) but it's usually much more modest.

It's found scattered throughout the upper *Abies* and hemlock forests in Sikkim and Bhutan and sometimes forms thickets or forests of its own at 6000–12,000 ft (1800–3600 m). In recent times it's also been found in Nepal and Assam, and is common in Arunachal Pradesh where it grows in lush mossy forests.

Some forms of the plant should be hardy given that Hooker found them growing on exposed mountain tops in Sikkim. The eternal problem is the early flowering and so the flowers are prone to frost damage. However, for a milder climate, it is one of the delights of the season and a stunning sight in full flower.

Because it was the first of the subsection to be discovered it is the 'type' species. It's the only one with a plastered silvery-grey to fawn indumentum.

Latin name means grand or large.
First Class Certificate 1901 from South Lodge, Horsham, UK
Hardiness rated at 2–3
Zone 9

> Joseph Hooker was the first to introduce this fine species but not the first to see or describe it. That honour goes to William Griffith who discovered it in Bhutan and it was subsequently described by Scottish botanist Robert Wight in 1847 in the *Calcutta Journal of Natural History*. Hooker then found it in Sikkim and named it *R. argenteum* (meaning silver), referring to the silvery undersides of the leaves. Wight's description said *R. grande* had fawn tomentum, so Hooker thought he had something different. In 1887 the two species were amalgamated.
>
> One of Hooker's original plants, introduced in 1850, is still growing at Stonefield Castle in Scotland. Hooker obviously thought it was special as he wrote:
>> '*Rhododendron dalhousiae* grows epiphytically, a slender shrub, bearing from three to six white lemon-scented bells, four and a half inches long and as many broad, at the end of each branch. In the same woods the scarlet rhododendron *R. arboreum* is very scarce, and is outvied by the great *R. argenteum*, which grows as a tree forty feet high, with magnificent leaves twelve to fifteen inches long, deep green, wrinkled above and silvery below, while the flowers are as large as those of *R. dalhousiae*, and grow more in a cluster. I know nothing of the kind that exceeds in beauty the flowering branch of *R. argenteum*, with its wide spreading foliage and glorious mass of flowers.'

R. kesangiae

(D.G. LONG AND RUSHFORTH, 1989)
Pronounced kess-ong-ee-ay

R. kesangiae var. *kesangiae* is an unusual and truly beautiful addition to the big-leafs. When I say addition, it's only been in cultivation since 1967 and was not classified as a new and separate species until 1989. It was introduced to the West in 1967 and thought to be a natural hybrid of *R. hodgsonii* x *R. falconeri*. As both of these are members of the Falconera subsection and both have smooth pale bark, it is surprising it took another twenty years to solve the mystery. Keith Rushforth realised it was different on his first Bhutan trip in 1985, but it was not in flower. His subsequent 1987 trip, in springtime, allowed him to collect many specimens, all with the same specific features and so was then able to confirm it as a new species. We now know it also grows further east, just in Arunachal Pradesh.

For many years the plants were thought to be *R. hodgsonii* x *R. falconeri* but neither of these parents have the rounded bud so typical of *R. kesangiae*. *R. hodgsonii* has smooth bronzy-purple

R. kesangiae at Meerkerk (top and middle) grown from the same batch of seed; and foliage at Pukeiti (bottom).

> Keith Rushforth describes how he became aware of this new species:
>
> 'October 1985 was my first trip to Bhutan. Right at the end I had a day on the Dochu La, west of Thimphu. David Lang was in the vicinity but the rest of the group were at a Buddhist festival in Thimphu. I remember the day well as we decided to leave our lunch under a bush as we went our separate ways, only for a dog to enjoy it! So much for remote mountain passes.
>
> I noted a dominant tree rhododendron in the Grandia alliance but it was sterile. A year later I was trying to get people together for a second trip — the first I led. Philippe de Spoelberch lent me his slides as he had been to Bhutan in the spring of 1985. What he was calling *R. hodgsonii* clearly was my Grandia — my seedling had round buds showing they were not *R. hodgsonii* and *R. grande* itself occurs below the *R. falconeri* zone, not above it. So before I went back to Bhutan in April/May 1987, I knew that there was a new species. On the '87 trip we did set about making sure that it wasn't *R. decipiens* and collected flowering specimens from the Dochu La to the Ura-Sheltang La. We noted that the flowers seemed a bit different on the Thrumsing La but the press was full. From about there, east to the Mande La area is where the *R. kesangiae* var. *album* occurs.'

As Keith suggests, this species is often found near the tops of mountain passes growing below a canopy of huge *Abies* and hemlock trees, above *R. falconeri* and below *R. hodgsonii* at 9000–11,500 ft (2700–3500 m), but overlapping with both. The surprise is the plant is so common and it's a puzzle as to why previous explorers never recognised it as being different. Griffith's description came when plants were not flowering, and perhaps the plant is described in Latin and buried in his script.

R. kesangiae at Pukeiti from seed from Bhutan (left), and growing in Bhutan (right).

trunks which peel, whereas *R. kesangiae* has rough bark and is often laden with moss, an attractive and a distinguishing feature as opposed to the trunks of *R. hodgsonii* and *R. falconeri*. There are, however, hybrids between *R. kesangiae* and the other two, found growing wild in Bhutan.

Typically 10–50 ft (3–15 m) tall with glorious leaves, obovate to broadly elliptic, usually 8–12 in (20–30 cm) long and 4–6 in (10–15 cm) wide with a rounded apex and long petioles. On top, they are rich dark green with prominent lateral veins and patches of white indumentum and a matt of silver-white, sometimes brown, indumentum beneath. The undersides are covered with a matted layer of hairs which can be almost woolly, but the hairs are not cup-shaped. The leaf buds are distinctive, being squat and round, often red or purple in colour, which is unlike other large-leaf species. The petioles are weak, causing the leaves to spin in strong winds and eventually break.

With its delightful heads of rich rosy-pink campanulate flowers, this is one of the best of the big-leafs for flower colour and all-round display. Some have really huge, densely packed heads and others are slightly open and floppy. The flowers vary, too, with some having a simple wavy edge and others are more crinkle cut. There are around fifteen to twenty flowers in each showy truss and they have nectar pouches and a crimson blotch in the base.

There is a white-flowered version found in eastern Bhutan, *R. kesangiae*, var. *album*, with showy white flowers with bright red nectaries in the base of the tube. The leaves are slightly different as well, with a shinier surface and more prominent veins. They flower in April to May and that's likely to be October in the southern hemisphere.

The plant is named after a member of the Bhutanese royal family, H.R.H. the Queen Mother, Kesang Dorjii Wangchuck (mother of the fourth king of Bhutan). Appropriately for the 'heavenly kingdom', this plant is truly celestial. The rich rosy-pink flowers are perhaps the best of all the big-leafs — they are literally crowd-stoppers. We had the privilege of seeing them in flower in Bhutan on the high passes, both on the Dochu La, and again on the Pele La in even greater abundance on an International Dendrology Society trip in 2004. There was a jaw-dropping moment followed by the repeated clicks of a dozen cameras.

Although these plants are relatively new to cultivation they are proving to be good garden plants. They are much hardier to cold than most of the big-leafs and seem generally more robust except for their being prone to wind damage. With the scintillating strong pink colour, they are likely to prove very popular in future.

Hardiness rated at 4

Zones 8–9

GRANDIA SUBSECTION

R. macabeanum

(WATT EX) BALF.F., 1920)
Pronounced mak-cabe-ee-anum

If you were new to the giant rhododendrons and wanted to start a collection then this is one of the best species to begin with. It's big, it's handsome, it's robust; and it's very easy to grow. Considering that most of the wild plants came from low altitudes, it has turned out to be surprisingly cold-hardy. Even more surprising, it is more tolerant of wind and drought than most.

In terms of sheer beauty it's probably in the top three and certainly the top five along with *R. protistum* and *R. kesangiae*. But then it's hard to leave out *R. sinogrande* or *R. sinofalconeri* and, and, and . . .

But it's certainly up there — maybe not the biggest leaf, or the tallest plant, but certainly one of the most fantastic rhododendrons. It has a chunky feet-on-the-ground look about it, like a sumo wrestler. As a flat-top tree, it's not trying to reach for the sky but rather to find a place on this earth. Like many trees and shrubs when brought into a warmer climate, they tend to be stockier, spreading rather than increasing in height.

The combination of glossy grey leaves and bright yellow flowers wins the heart of any who see it in bloom. Another winning trait is its ability to flower as a young plant, so you are not waiting decades for a flower. Many forms have fabulous silver-grey indumentum beneath, and the young growth and branchlets are smothered in white woolly indumentum. When the new growth emerges, it is like an altar of pointy red candles. When mature, the rich green leaves have obvious veins or ribbing and a prominent yellow midrib. Often the leaves are a narrow elliptical shape but they can be huge paddles 13 in (33 cm) long and 8 in (20 cm) wide. The adult foliage is surprisingly tough, tolerating windy and colder sites better than most other species.

Fabulous primrose-yellow domes of funnel-shaped to campanulate flowers 8–9 in (20–23 cm) across packed with about fifteen to thirty flowers are perfection. Some forms are pale yellow or closer to white and most have a purple blotch contrasting the main colour. The majority of

R. macabeanum showing new foliage growth.

R. macabeanum at Brodick, Scotland (below, left) and leaves, at Pukeiti (below, right).

Opposite: *R. macabeanum* at Pukeiti.

R. macabeanum at Pukeiti.

The first plants in cultivation came from near the summit of Mt Japvo in Nagaland, altitude 9892 ft (3015 m), and were collected by Kingdon Ward in 1927, and again on several occasions further to the east. Kingdon Ward described it as being common in places and covering mountain tops in almost pure stands.

Kingdon Ward is often credited with discovering the plant but that honour in fact goes to Sir George Watt (1851–1930), a Scottish surgeon who was sent to India to teach but found himself in a party surveying the proposed boundary between Nagaland and Burma. He found the plant in 1882 and named it after his good friend Robert Blair McCabe (1854–1897) who was Deputy Commissioner and Inspector-General of the Police in Nagaland. When he first arrived in India, McCabe was sent to the Naga Hills where his mission was to pacify the fierce tribes of the district. A tricky task given the locals were head-hunters and his predecessor had just been murdered. In between mundane paperwork and life-threatening revolts he managed to spend time studying local plants. He was highly regarded for his bravery and his diplomacy, often saving lives with either a few soothing words or, if need be, a wave of his pistol. Tragically, he died when his house collapsed in an earthquake on 12 June 1897. He was just forty-three years old. Had he survived he would have received the Order of the Star of India for bravery as mentioned on the front page of the *London Gazette*, 29 June 1897.

The true discoverer of the plant, Sir George Watt, wrote a colossal twelve-volume *Dictionary of Economic Products of India*, and retired to Scotland. He also discovered a natural hybrid, known for many years as *R. wattii*, but now recognised to be a natural cross *arboreum* × *macabeanum*, as they, along with *R. burmanicum*, are the only species in the region as determined by Steve Hootman.

Probably the best form is KW 7724. It has won several awards.

Award of Merit, 1937. AM form with blotched flowers.

First Class Certificate, 1938. FCC form has pure yellow flowers. Both clones from Trengwainton, Cornwall, England.

AGM 1984. RHS Award of Garden Merit.

Hardiness rated at 3–4

Zones 8–9

plants available for sale are seedlings, but if possible try to find grafted plants and preferably a good clear yellow form. Flowers appear from March to May (September to October). One of its good habits is that it flowers as a young plant rather than taking decades, as some species do when grown from seed. It also hybridises with other rhododendrons; seed from cultivated plants often spring surprises when they flower, so should not be treated as true species.

Because it flowers fairly early in the season, one needs to choose a very sheltered site not prone to heavy frosts. Find enough shade to keep the frosts at bay and avoid east-facing sites exposed to early morning sun, which exacerbates frost damage. The plant itself is fairly hardy to cold and frosts but they do perform better in mild climates. In the wild, the tree grows at altitudes of 8000–12,000 ft (2400–3700 m), so there should be hardier forms available. In recent times, Steve Hootman (Executive Director of the Rhododendron Species Foundation) has found them around 12,000 ft (3700 m) on Mt Saramati in Nagaland, north-eastern India and has distributed these higher altitude forms. Hopefully these will prove much hardier.

It is native to Manipur and also the Naga Hills of Nagaland in north-east India and possibly into Burma.

R. magnificum at Pukeiti (above, left and right).

R. magnificum

(KINGDON WARD, 1935)
Pronounced mag-nif-i-cum

Both this and the closely related *R. protistum* are the most tender types within the Grandia subsection. Although they are very similar, *R. magnificum* usually has longer, narrower leaves, and the indumentum appears on much younger plants than with *R. protistum*.

How, then, does the plant behave in cultivation? It's an extra-large shrub or small tree but only suited to very sheltered woodland gardens. The plant needs protection from strong winds and early frosts because the flowers emerge in winter. As it is often one of the earliest to flower, this can be a real problem in frosty areas — February through to April (July to September) is typical.

The name *magnificum* is very appropriate given the oblanceolate leaves can be 12–30 in (30–76 cm) long, but these reduce with age to half that size. They are narrow, elliptic, dark green with a slight sheen on the upper surface with greyish-fawn indumentum beneath. Indumentum is lacking in early years and when it does appear it's usually as a narrow marginal band underneath. This widens in successive years until the whole underside appears covered. This happens much earlier than with *R. protistum*, which may take twenty-five years or more. Flowering rarely occurs before the appearance of indumentum under the leaf. Terminal growth buds are characteristically purple-red at the tips, as well as tall and pointy, all of which are indicators of the species.

R. magnificum at Pukeiti showing new growth emerging.

Emerging new growth is decked in long red strands as the protective bracts peel away, revealing the new silvery-green leaves, a visual bonus. Even though the plant flowers early in the season, the new growth, by comparison, seems to be late arriving, which is good in cold regions.

The flower heads are impressive with twelve up to twenty-five flowers in a racemose umbel which usually has less per truss than *R. protistum*. In good forms, the flower heads are huge balls of fuchsia pink, while some are white through to rosy-purple with darker nectar pouches. Often a washed-out pink has a deep-red interior, but is still very attractive. The big bell or tubular campanulate-shaped flowers are packed into a dense truss, making it all the more appealing, but still not as dense as *R. protistum*. The waxy texture of the flowers makes them more resistant to weather damage, other than frost.

Like most big-leafs, they take a few years to flower, perhaps a little longer than most at between twenty to thirty-five years, but not as long as *R. protistum*.

Award of Merit for foliage, 1950, Corsewell, Stranraer, Scotland to KW 9200.

First Class Certificate, 1966, to clone 'Kildonan', KW 9200, Brodick Castle, Isle of Arran, Scotland. A dense dome form with fuchsia-pink flowers.

Hardiness rated at 1–3

Zone 9

R. magnificum was first discovered in the remote hills of far north Burma by Frank Kingdon Ward in 1931 under the collection number KW 9200, and again as 9301 and 9213. He was in the Adung Long Valley at an elevation of 5000–8000 ft (1500–2400 m). One tree was so incredibly big — he reckoned around 50 ft (15 m) with a 3 ft (1 m) diameter trunk, at head height. Even more incredible, he estimated the tree was covered in 1000 flower heads. Now that's 'magnificum' — what else could he call it. The tree was officially named and published by him in 1935. It's only ever been found in that north Burma region, bordering on Tibet. There must be so many more plants to discover in that part of the country, but no one has really worked in there since Kingdon Ward. He found it at elevations ranging from 5000–8000 ft (1500–2400 m), where it occurred primarily in forests.

His description is enough to excite any rhodophile: 'In February the dark forest is lit up explosively by its immense trusses of rosy purple, crimson purple and carmine purple blossoms. This great hearted rhododendron forms much of the lower tier of forest and is especially common all along the cliffs overhanging the river.'

Unfortunately this region is off limits these days, and the other drawback is that Kingdon Ward says the trees are only just above the tropical zone which would account for the flowers in February. It is likely the species exists in nearby regions of Tibet and Arunachal Pradesh. Ken Cox and Steve Hootman found plants growing in nearby Arunachal Pradesh in October 2003 that seemed to fit some of the parameters of *R. magnificum*.

R. montroseanum

(DAVIDIAN, 1979)
Pronounced mont-rose-ee-anum

The oblanceolate, glossy leaves are glorious, with impressed veining giving a bullate appearance, and growing up to 30 in (76 cm), but half that size with age. The leaves often droop down when conditions are cold or excessively dry. They are a very handsome rich dark shiny green on top and have a soft silver-white indumentum beneath, later becoming shiny silvery-bronze. The wedge-shaped leaves are rounded at the tips, and they often droop or roll cigar-fashion from stress. The plants can be sparse-looking because they don't hold their leaves for long, usually one or two seasons. New growth appears in May as silvery-white spears. The plant makes an upright shrub up to 30 ft (9 m) in cultivation.

The flowers are equally wonderful and they are a distinguishing factor from other species. Opening to a round ball of vibrant rich pink and gradually fading to softer or very pale pink, it is quite different to *R. grande* and *R. sinograde*. Up to twenty flowers packed in the head make it a display to remember. The truss is a racemose umbel of fifteen to twenty oblique campanulate, eight-lobed flowers with no nectar pouches.

Flowers appear in February and March (August to September) and with new growth in May (October), which can be a real problem in colder regions. Try to find a warm sheltered site for this magnificent plant.

Benmore F.C.C. form of *R. montroseanum* at Pukeiti (above) and (below), showing new foliage.

The species remains one of the few not found anywhere else and which has not been seen or collected again until very recently. The initial recording of it as *R. sinograde* was reinforced by Kenneth Cox when retracing Kingdon Ward's expedition in 1995. He found *R. sinograde* growing abundantly with another, *R. lanigerum*, which

R. montroseanum Benmore F.C.C. form at Pukeiti.

is red-flowered. The hybridising of these two species has probably produced what we know as *R. montroseanum*, now well established and breeding true. It still remains rare in cultivation and most plants have been derived from seed from the 'Brodick' form or 'Benmore' form.

First Class Certificate, 1957 to 'Benmore' KW 6261A clone, Younger Botanic Gardens, Benmore, Scotland.

The plant illustrated was grown from seed from the 'Benmore' clone from the American Rhododendron Society seed exchange. Hardiness rated at 2–3

Zone 9

> What a wonderful and well-deserved honour for the Duchess of Montrose to have this fabulous tree named after her. The Duchess was the daughter of the Hamiltons who owned Brodick Castle in Scotland for generations. This species was initially called *R. mollyanum* and was later changed to *R. montroseanum* in 1979, long after the death of Mary, Duchess of Montrose, who died in 1957. But the plant *was* named after her, in fact, as her family and close friends called her Molly. The reason for the change was that someone had named a New Guinea Vireya rhododendron as *R. mollianum* back in 1909 and that name takes precedence, by date.
>
> At Brodick, the Duchess created much of the garden, as can be seen in the distinctive design, a style so recognisably hers. It was during her era that the garden acquired a stunning collection of newly introduced rhododendrons, fruits of Forrest and Kingdon Ward's efforts as they combed the mountains of Asia for new species. Kingdon Ward collected *R. montroseanum* in 1924 at a relatively low altitude of 8000–9000 ft (2400–2700 m). This was in the Tsangpo Gorge in southern Tibet under the collector's number KW 6261A. One only had to mention the word Tibet to British gardeners of a certain age and they would go all misty-eyed. Thanks to men like Kingdon Ward, Sir Francis Younghusband and Heinrich Harrer, and the books they wrote, there was an army of armchair explorers trying to picture themselves high in the mountains and valleys of Tibet, scouring the land for new plants.

R. praestans

(BALF.F. AND W.W.SM., 1916)
Pronounced pray-stans

Above: *R. praestans* Exbury form from seed, and possibly a hybrid, at Pukeiti.

For anyone wanting to start a big-leaf collection *R. praestans* is a great place to start as it's fairly easy to grow. Experts agree this species is tougher than most, tolerating more wind, exposure and cold weather than most of its relatives. And it's a handsome, rewarding plant. With big, bold, rich-green shiny leaves, it looks important and imposing. As a distinguishing feature, the oblanceolate to obovate leaf tapers into a winged and flattened short petiole. The upper surface is dark green, slightly indented to give a bubbled appearance. The undersides are coated with a thin layer of shiny indumentum, usually dark brown on a young plant but can be silver, changing to fawn as the plant ages. These leaves can be enormous, up to 18 in (45 cm) long on a young plant, but half of that on a mature plant, and the bush can grow to 30 ft (9 m). The plant tends to be broader than it is high, with rough trunks, sometimes with mottled bark. It is usually a well-clothed shrub, dense in habit but very slow-growing and slow to reach flowering size.

The obliquely campanulate flowers appear in a dense racemose umbel of fifteen to twenty-five eight-lobed flowers in spring — March to May in the northern hemisphere and August to September in the south. The tight truss of flowers are typically magenta or pink but can be white or pale yellow, often with a crimson blotch inside and without nectar pouches. There are really good whites and pinks available but many forms are just plain muddy. The trusses of flower are flat-topped, dense and tight, adding to their appeal.

Left, top and bottom: *R. praestans*.

This species was discovered and introduced by George Forrest in 1914. He was on a journey up into north-west Yunnan and south-east Tibet and found this on the Mekong–Yangtze divide. Its home is up around 9000–14,000 ft (2700–4300 m) in dry, open pine forests. Perhaps this is why the plant is tougher than most, because it has to cope with harsh conditions in its native habitat.

R. praestans readily hybridises in the wild with other species and *R. rothschildii* and *R. semnoides* are two that have probably become stable populations from this common ancestor.

R. coryphaeum is now regarded as a synonym of *R. praestans*. The flowers are creamy-white with rich red interior. Usually flowers in April. Introduced in 1918 by George Forrest.

In Latin, *praestans* means distinguished or excelling, and *coryphaeum* means crown or head.

Award of Merit, 1963 to clone 'Exbury' and has pale yellow flowers with a crimson blotch and was exhibited as *R. coryphaeum* by the Exbury Gardens in Hampshire, England.

Hardiness rated at 3–4

Zones 8–9

R. protistum var. *protistum*
(BALF.F. AND FORREST, 1920)
INCLUDING *R. PROTISTUM* VAR. *GIGANTEUM* (FORREST EX TAGG,)
D.F.CHAMBERLAIN 1979
Pronounced pro-tist-um

R. protistum Hillier form at Pukeiti.

Huge leaves the size of a forearm deck this plant. The top surface is a matt finish and not shiny. There is no indumentum on the young leaves and they can be double the adult size. At the juvenile stage, a year or two before flowering, each leaf develops a narrow band of indumentum round the edge which then fills in and covers the entire underside once the plant is mature. It now appears this is the juvenile form and *R. p.* var. *giganteum* is the adult form of the same species. In the early days of Forrest's collections these two were perceived to be different, but as the trees have matured people have realised they are both one species, or synonymous.

In the wild they can reach phenomenal heights, some estimated to be over 100 ft (30 m). In cultivation it grows to 45 ft (14 m) high and can be more than 60 ft (18 m) across if grown in

Left: *R. protistum* in north-west Yunnan.

the open. Typically found in lush mixed forests around 8500–9000 ft (2600–2700 m).

The rich dark-green paddle-like obovate to elliptic leaves can be up to 18 in (45 cm) long on a mature plant, and as much as 30 in (76 cm) on a juvenile plant. They have a rich green matt surface and prominent veins below. Juvenile leaves have no indumentum while the mature leaves appear smooth underneath but often have a thin webbing of indumentum, a sign of maturity and flower production. The growth can be early in spring and there is the ever-present risk of frost. An added attraction to the emergence of the new leaves is the host of bright red leaf scales.

Flowers form a large racemose umbel and vary in size and colour, but can be anything from creamy-white through various shades of pink including a rich sensuous pink, red and purple. Many are spotted within or have a deep crimson blotch with nectar pouches.

The dense heads have thirty or more oblique campanulate flowers often with darker nectar pouches at the base. Unfortunately, the flowers appear early in the season, February to March in the northern hemisphere, July to August in the southern and are therefore prone to frost damage. This magnificent plant needs a mild climate and a sheltered site to perform at its peak, but when it does, it really is the best.

> The original *R. protistum* var. *protistum* was discovered by George Forrest in 1918 in west Yunnan near the Burmese border. It's possible to see them now in the Gaoligongshan National Nature Reserve, and along the Dulong Jiang River in western Yunnan.
>
> The most magnificent tree rhododendron I've ever seen is a form of *R. protistum* var. *giganteum*. This specimen was grown from seed collected by Kingdon Ward in Burma in 1953 on one of his last trips. After trial, the best seedling was named 'Pukeiti' after the garden where it now grows. The seedlings didn't flower until 1974 but they've made up for it since with masses of blooms nearly every year. KW 21498 was collected in the far north of Burma, slightly towards China, and on the Burmese side of the Gaoligongshan mountain. This form is undoubtedly one of the best big-leafs you're ever likely to see and should be in every major collection, if climate allows.

Latin *protistum* means first or best.

Hardiness rated at 1–3

Zone 9

GRANDIA SUBSECTION

R. protistum var. *giganteum*
(FORREST EX TAGG) D.F.CHAMBERLAIN 1979
Pronounced ji-gant-eum

R. protistum 'Pukeiti' at Pukeiti.

Latin *giganteum* means gigantic.

First Class Certificate 1953 from Brodick Castle, Isle of Arran, Scotland.

Hardiness rated at 1–3

Zone 9

The leaves on a young plant are enormous, oval to elliptic, up to 28 x 12 in (70 x 30 cm) but perhaps only half this size when mature. The top surface is rich matt green with indented veins and below it is pale, initially without any indumentum. This juvenile phase can last for years, but one year a thin marginal fawn indumentum will appear on the new leaves which will spread across the underside of the leaf with each new growth phase, eventually leading to fully indumented leaves. Often all three stages of indumentum can be seen on a plant at one time, making the distinction of the two species dubious. Supposedly the difference between the two forms is that *R. protistum* var. *giganteum* has a continuous layer of thin greyish-buff indumentum on the lower leaf surface. Some experts believe this is the adult form of *R. protistum* var. *protistum* because the tree can take decades before it's fully clothed in indumentum. The new growth is very attractive with red bud scales which peel back from the emerging silver spears.

BIG-LEAF RHODODENDRONS

The heads of twenty to thirty oblique campanulate flowers have dark nectar pouches. The flowers vary from pink to rose, red or purple and are invariably very beautiful. Some forms have enormous flower heads the size of a soccer ball. The sixteen stamens are unequal in length, but always shorter than the corolla tube.

In New Zealand, the mild conditions advance the flowering stage with the plant often blooming after twenty years, though it can take over thirty-five years. Unfortunately, the plant is not hardy and will only grow in very warm sheltered gardens. Another drawback is the early flowering in February to March (July to August) which can be problematic in frosty areas.

> The species was originally known as *R. giganteum* and now we use the name in a historical sense because although it has been merged with *R. protistum* it is still known and labelled as *R. giganteum* in many collections around the world. In the wild it is the tallest of the big-leafs and possibly the tallest rhododendrons in the world, competing with a few *R. arboreum* in the mountains of Manipur. George Forrest was the first to find this in the wild in 1919 in south-west Yunnan, when he discovered some trees he estimated its height to be 80 ft (24 m). Forrest came across it again in north-west Yunnan and north-east Burma and claimed one of these later finds was 100 ft (30 m) tall. In cultivation it's more likely to be a wide-spreading large shrub because it's not drawn upwards by the light.

R. protistum new growth at Pukeiti.

R. pudorosum

(COWAN, 1937)

Pronounced pude-or-osum

An unusual plant with handsome shiny leaves, slightly rugose and silvery below and with bright pink trumpet flowers. At first glance this doesn't look like it belongs in this subsection.

The tree can grow to 40 ft (12 m) but is much more compact in cultivation and the leaves up to 14 in (35 cm). The unusual aspect is the shiny, rich green leaves, which make it look more like something from the *R. fortunei* subsection. The underside of the leaves has a very thin silver indumentum. The persistent leaf bud scales are a distinguishing feature, lasting for several years, giving a shaggy appearance unlike any other large-leaf rhododendron.

Another surprise is that the bright pink flowers are scented. There's often a purple blotch within the flower but there are no nectar pouches. The truss is quite tidy and dense, making a good show in February to March (August to September).

Coming from southern Tibet at around 11,000–12,500 ft (3300–3800 m) where it grows in *Abies* forests, it was first collected by Ludlow and Sherriff in 1936 under LS 2752. It's not common in the wild and is considered a very rare plant in cultivation. Coming from higher altitudes makes it more hardy, so it is worth seeking out, although the early flowering still means a sheltered position in the garden.

Latin *puderosum* means reluctant or bashful in reference to the flowers. It seems to be reluctant to flower, taking thirty-six years for the first plants to bloom. It had only been collected the once until a reintroduction by Ken Cox in 1999 from south-east Tibet and many young plants grown from this seed are now in cultivation.

Hardiness rated at 3–4

Zones 7–9

R. sidereum at Pukeiti.

R. sidereum

(BALF.F., 1920)
Pronounced sid-eer-eum

Naturally found in mixed forest in the mountains between the top part of Burma and western Yunnan at 8000–13,000 ft (2500–4000 m). In effect this is the Chinese version of *R. grande* but the leaves are reduced in size, making it hardier and more tolerant of extremes. These smaller leaves are plastered in similar silvery indumentum like *R. grande* and are matt green above. In general it's regarded as the hardier of the two given it has smaller leaves but they do come from similar altitudes. Although it is closely related to *R. grande*, it flowers much later, which is advantageous in cold climates.

R. sidereum foliage (above) and flower heads (below) at Pukeiti.

The flowers vary from creamy-white to shades of yellow or pale pink, usually with a small red eye or larger blotch. Not the most exciting of flowers but some clones have good colour and tend to hold that colour rather than fade. It's worth seeking out the better yellow-flowering clones. Typically there are twelve to twenty flowers in a good-sized truss but some clones can be small and not very showy.

It does have several endearing features. Flowers appear in May or even June (November) which is a blessing and another reason to grow it as the chance of being hit by frost is slim. It even has a reputation for resisting root rots in warmer climes. Often has a very upright habit, with leaves and habit like an *R. arboreum*.

In Latin, *sidereum* means excellent.

Hardiness rated at 2–3

Zone 9

There is a good cultivar called 'Glen Rosa' with primrose-yellow flowers and a deep crimson blotch within which won an Award of Merit in 1964 from Brodick Castle, Scotland.

R. sidereum was discovered by a Captain Abbey in 1912 in north-east Burma and both Reginald Farrer and George Forrest introduced it to cultivation in 1919. Some forms are quite small and the small leaves do not look like a big-leaf rhododendron at all.

R. sinogrande
(BALF.F. & W.W.SM., 1916)
Pronounced sino-grand-ee

First discovered near his Tenchong base by George Forrest in 1912 and introduced by him. Nowadays they can be found in Gaoligongshan National Nature Reserve, western China. Kingdon Ward said it grew up to 50 ft (15 m) high and created an almost pure understorey to *Tsuga* in Assam. What a sight that must be.

In more recent times, Tom Hudson and Steve Hootman found a 75 ft (23 m) specimen in the Dulong Valley, north-west Yunnan in 2000.

R. sinogrande at Pukeiti.

R. *sinogrande* at Pukeiti.

The granddaddy of them all, *R. sinogrande* has the largest leaves of any rhododendron and is undoubtedly the biggest and the best of the genus. Nothing can match the enormous leaves of this fabulous species. They are usually a rich bottle-green and as shiny as a Rolls-Royce.

There are forms with a matt finish, but either one is delightful. The bold yellow veining only adds to the appeal. To complete the perfect picture, the underside is completely covered in a thin layer of silvery or fawn indumentum. The oblanceolate to elliptic leaves can be up to 3 ft (91 cm) long and 1 ft (30 cm) wide, quite thick and leathery, and the overall span of a crown of leaves can be an imposing umbrella-like tree. It looks so tropical, as if it should be native to the Amazon rather than the cold mountains of western China.

Flowers form a racemose umbel and are very impressive, too, with a dome of fifteen to thirty bell-shaped oblique campanulate flowers up to 9 in (22 cm) across. Some forms have a wide flat-topped truss. The flowers appear from March to May (October to November) and are usually ivory-white, cream or pale yellow or sometimes true yellow, usually with a crimson blotch in the base of the flower. The true yellow forms are the most desirable. The waxy flowers are held at oblique angles, spacing them neatly in the truss, and each has dark nectar pouches.

Like so many of the giant rhododendrons, they tend to bear flowers every other year, sometimes taking a two-year rest between flowerings. Deadheading after flowering helps them flower every year.

This species is instantly recognisable because of the huge leaves, and also because of the silvery indumentum beneath. Hardiness is a problem, and not only cold temperatures but strong winds can damage or debilitate the plant. In the Pacific north-west USA, it is heavily damaged or sometimes killed at 10°F (−12°C) so choose as sheltered a spot as you can find for this luxuriant beauty. And it goes without saying, a misty moist climate is what it needs to show off all its glory. Plants can be gaunt and open but they improve with age and become tree-like, growing to 38 ft (12 m) in sheltered conditions.

The tree hails from western Yunnan and also south-east Tibet, upper Burma, Arunachal Pradesh and Assam at around 7000–11,500 ft (2000–3500 m) but usually at the lower end of those altitudes. Depending on the altitude plants or seeds were collected, the progeny are of variable hardiness. But, regardless, they need a sheltered moist site to perform well.

Most forms are susceptible to late frost, damaging both flowers and growth buds. There is a high altitude form var. *boreale* which has proven to be hardier, with smaller leaves and flowers, but it is still uncommon in cultivation.

The Latin *sinogrande* means Chinese *grande*.

Award of Merit, 1922, to South Lodge, Sussex, England.

First Class Certificate, 1926, to Trewithen, Cornwall, England.

Hardiness rated at 1–3

Zone 9

GRANDIA SUBSECTION

R. suoilenhense at Pukeiti.

R. suoilenhense

(D.F. CHAMBERLAIN AND K. RUSHFORTH)
Pronounced swoe-lin-ense

Great plant — pity about the tongue-twister name. I'm told it's named after a mountain peak, Mt Suoilen near the town of Sapa in the very north of Vietnam. It was first discovered in 1991 in the Lao Cai province in the northern part of Vietnam at 7000–10,300 ft (2100–3100 m). Discovered by Tom Hudson, Keith Rushforth and Alan Clark and initially described as a *R. grande* type resembling both *protistum* and *sinograde*. Luckily it flowers at a young age and it was soon realised this was a new species.

Later another population was found growing on Mt Tay Con Linh, north and east of the Red River, very close to the Chinese border. It is found around 7500–8000 ft (2200–2400 m) growing with *Tsuga dumosa*, *Sorbus* sp. and members of the Fagaceae and Lauraceae families.

In the wild, it's a tree, growing to 50 ft (15 m) with bold, broadly oblong leaves up to 12–16 in (30–40 cm) long.

Young plants have huge shiny leaves, looking more like an Amazon jungle plant rather than a rhododendron. The upper surface on juvenile plants is bright glossy green. Below, the leaves are matt green and initially have no indumentum at all, and then an outer marginal band of indumentum develops, eventually covering the whole underside on a mature plant in much the same way as *R. protistum*. The juvenile leaves are thin and often have a wavy, undulating edge.

Leaves on older plants are thicker and very shiny on top and the leaf shape changes to become elliptic and smaller. It was thought to be a *R. protistum* affinity at first, but is different in that the indumentum develops on young plants. Coming into new growth late in spring means less damage by frosts.

The almost dainty heads of white flowers usually have a noticeable crimson red blotch within. Some have a marvellous strawberry red centre. The trusses are packed with flowers which vary slightly in colour, some clones being more cream or dirty white. The flowers are fleshy, tubular campanulate, fifteen to twenty with eight lobes and held in a loose truss. There are sixteen stamens and the ovary is densely covered with white hairs. In some forms the flowers appear to be too small compared to the huge leaves, as if the two are not in proportion. Flowers mostly resemble *R. sinogrande* but on a smaller scale.

Two features which will appeal to gardeners are that the leaves are huge big bold glossy paddles; and the plant flowers very early in life. Often the first flowers appear within five to eight years as opposed to some like *R. protistum* which can take fifty years.

A very vigorous plant, early indications are it is reasonably hardy. Another factor is the later May (October) flowering season. This late flowering means the blooms are less likely to be frosted. Initially, it's easy to imagine that everything from Vietnam must be semi-tropical and not hardy but that's not always the case. Many forms of plants such as *R. nuttallii* and *R. excellens* from Vietnam are hardier than more northern populations. Possibly this is because cold air is forced down from the north during winter and squeezed towards south-east China and Vietnam by the Himalayan massif. In the case of this species, it's proving to be much hardier than first imagined.

Hardiness rated at 1–3, more likely 2–3.

Zone 9

R. suoilenhense at Pukeiti (left and right).

R. watsonii.

R. watsonii

(HEMSL. AND E.H.WILSON, 1910)
Pronounced wat-sone-ii

It's ironic that you find the species which is tougher and more resilient than most of its peers, then have it turn out to be the least attractive of the group. *R. watsonii* grows in dry conifer forests in western Sichuan around 9000–11,000 ft (2700–3300 m). These tough conditions have hardened the plant and turned it into a survivor. It's been in cultivation a long time, since 1908, and was first discovered by Ernest Wilson but remains very rare in cultivation. Despite its natural growing conditions it does remain susceptible to frosted flowers and new growth.

As a tree it can grow to 20 ft (6 m) but it's usually much less than this. The leaves can be 13 in (33 cm) long, but again usually much less and the short, slightly winged petioles make the leaves seem smaller. The surface of the leaf is a dull pale green, possibly the least exciting of the subsection but some forms have very attractive glossy leaves. The leaves do have a prominent V-shaped yellow midrib, thicker at the base. Underneath is a plastered silvery indumentum which is often glabrous for many years. The smooth ovary is what separates it from others in the subsection, but from a gardener's perspective it looks more like an everyday hybrid rhododendron than a member of the illustrious Grandia subsection and is probably a hybrid that has stabilised.

The flowers tend to be in a ten to sixteen truss, muddy white, sometimes with a hint of pink. There are some really nice pure white forms and soft pink clones in cultivation and it's worth seeking out the best of these. The flowering season is variable, ranging from March to May (August to October) and the later clones would be better in a colder area. Its downfall is that it is often reluctant to flower regularly.

Ernest Wilson named it after his friend and travelling companion Mr W.C. Haines-Watson, who was a British customs agent based in China.

Hardiness rated at H 4

Zones 7–9

R. species nova — R. balangense
(W.P. FANG, 1983)

This new species is found only on Balang Shan, 14,700 ft (4487 m), Sichuan, and as far north as you could expect a big-leaf rhododendron to grow, given the climate further north. It was found in a part of the Wolong Panda Reserve. Some botanists regard it as a hybrid, but despite that, the seedlings from seed collected in the wild are remarkably consistent and similar to each other. If it is a hybrid, then a likely parent is *R. watsonii*. The other parent is a mystery but could be *R. longesquamatum* which does have persistent bud scales, a distinguishing feature of *R. balangense*. *R. balangense* is also easily recognised by the winged petiole of the handsome foliage and often have a yellow midrib like *R. watsonii* but with a greyish loose woolly indumentum below.

The loose trusses of flowers are pink and white, sometimes seemingly striped in the young stages. Trusses carry thirteen to fifteen flowers, fairly open and loose and unusually have only ten stamens instead of the normal twelve to twenty. At present it is very rare in cultivation, but is likely to become far more popular as it's so cold-hardy. This fact alone will encourage people as it will allow gardeners in regions previously unable to grow big-leafs to dare to grow them.

Although described as a new species by W.P. Fang in the 1980s, it is now included in the Taliensia subsection by some botanists.

Hardiness rated at 4–5

R. balangense.

CHAPTER 6
Hybrids

Over the years the big-leaf rhododendrons have unwittingly built up a mystique. They are seen as wondrous plants from distant lands, conjuring up visions of Buddhist temples and stukkas perched high on misty mountains. Often there's a story of hardship attached to the plant as the original discoverer was kidnapped or pursued by bloodthirsty locals. At the very least, they were cold and hungry, fending off leeches and other biting creatures.

Someone then decides to take the pollen from a cultivated version of the plant and pop it on the stigma of a related species. Within a few years the resulting plants are thriving and, hopefully, within ten years they are flowering. Now, to the uninitiated, the flowers of this offspring are not going to look hugely different to either of the parents, and so they would be happy to have any one of the three plants in their garden. To the purists, however, the idea of growing hybrids is an anathema.

But if the average garden visitor is unable to distinguish between a true species and a hybrid, and is quite happy to enjoy them both regardless of parentage, then perhaps we should all simply enjoy the plant. I have a debateable *R. magnificum* in my garden, and while it looks ever more likely it is a hybrid, it still puts on a fantastic show every spring and displays its handsome leaves all year. I would prefer it had a history, the snowy mountain, leeches etc., but I am, nevertheless, content that I'm able to grow such a magnificent plant.

And never mind the pedigree of the plants, look at the pedigree of the plant-breeders who have hybridised big-leaf regal rhododendrons. Some of the best gardeners in the world and rhododendron fanatics have hybridised giant rhododendrons. People such as Sir Edmund and his son Sir Giles Loder, Lionel de Rothschild and his son Edmund, John Basford at Brodick Castle, David Leach and Hjalmar Larson in the USA and in New Zealand Graham Smith, Bernard Hollard and brothers Felix and Les Jury are just a few of them.

R. 'Barbara Hayes' (opposite) and new foliage, *R.* 'Jack Anderson', (above).

It didn't take long for people to begin hybridising big-leaf rhododendrons. Well, it must have been irresistible suddenly having two of these brand new giants in flower at the same time. The first recorded crosses between two big-leafs were done by John (J.T.) Boscawen (1820–1889, a clergyman who lived in Cornwall and co-founded the Tregothnan gardens) in 1860 when he crossed *R. grande* x *R. falconeri* ssp. *falconeri* to create the 'Elsae' group' or grex. In this case, *R. grande* is the female parent and always comes first when we look at plant parentage.

It's a measure of the considerable esteem in which friends and family are held that breeders name big-leaf rhododendrons after them. These same breeders and selectors could easily attach these family names to popular hybrids of more modest dimensions, which would make them better known, but prefer instead to choose the 'select' or choice big-leafs, an indication of how venerated the giant-leaf versions are.

It should be remembered that the number of gardens growing these majestic rhododendrons around the world is relatively small so it follows that the degree to which hybridising is undertaken would be limited because they will never be commercial plants. Modern living in cities and urban areas with ever decreasing garden spaces means that only a few keen growers will want new hybrid large-leaf rhododendrons, particularly if the old adage of 'hybrid vigour' is taken into consideration. The thought of two 10-metre tall parents producing even bigger, more vigorous offspring gives cause for apprehension. Thankfully, however, you can seldom stop a hybridist from trying something new and we will see more large-leafs crossed with small rhododendrons, just to see what happens and just, maybe, a real winner will appear.

R. 'Gordon Collier' at Pukeiti.

'Barbara Hayes'

R. hodgsonii x *R. grande*

A delightful pink flower with a crenulated edge to the corolla. This true rich pink fades to cream as the truss ages. Brought back as seed from a plant found on a steep bank in Sikkim by Des Hayes, New Zealand, and raised by Bruce Campbell in Dunedin. Ron Gordon, who led the tour in question, initially thought it a *R. grande* but obviously it is a hybrid because it fits exactly halfway between two species — the flower shape and colouring are like *R. hodgsonii* but the leaves and bark are closer to *R. grande*, though it does have whiskers on the buds like *R. hodgsonii*. The location also fits perfectly because it was growing 650 ft (200 m) above the main *R. grande* population and 650 ft (200 m) below that of *R. hodgsonii*.

'Charles'

R. falconeri ssp. *falconeri* x *R. sinograndei*

A Lionel de Rothschild hybrid registered by his son Edmund in 1983. A dense head of flowers in off-white or champagne with a deep purple red throat. Leaves have handsome indumentum beneath.

A sister seedling named 'Annapolis Royal', for the city in Nova Scotia, has very pale green flowers with pink striping and dense woolly indumentum beneath. This is just one of several in the 'Fortune' grex or sister seedlings that the Rothschilds have named from Exbury Gardens.

'Churchill'

R. falconeri ssp. *falconeri* x *R. sinograndei*

An Edmund de Rothschild hybrid named after the wartime leader. Another example of how big-leaf hybrids are named after important people. The plant favours *R. falconeri*, having thick brown indumentum and pale primrose-yellow flowers.

Award of Merit RHS, 1971

'Colonel Rogers'

R. falconeri ssp. *falconeri* x *R. niveum*

Bred by Colonel Rogers in 1926, it is a strong plant with appealing white flowers edged in purple-pink creating a frilly feminine look. Interesting to use *R. niveum* as a parent, but it would be the deep dense purple trusses that attracted.

Above, top and bottom: *R.* 'Barbara Hayes'.

R. 'Colonel Rogers'.

There are at least two forms of this around, one being a purple-pink and less attractive. A photo taken on the Isle of Gigha, Scotland is of the original clone from the Colonel's garden. The Horlick family, who were close friends of the Colonel, owned the island and probably took the original plant with them when they moved there from the south-east of England.

'Crarae'

R. niveum x unknown

Raised at Crarae Gardens, Scotland, this has tight neat trusses of soft mauve and narrow leaves with whitish indumentum below. An unusual colour on an open-growing medium-sized shrub.

'Elsae'

R. grande x *R. hodgsonii*

A rather classy bush and flower with opaque ivory-like flowers, each with a purple throat. Dark green leaves with thin indumentum. Raised by the Reuthe Nursery near London before 1925, when it received an Award of Merit.

Admiral Algernon Walker-Heneage-Vivian at Clyne Castle did the same cross in 1933 and used the grex name of Clyne for several clones including another 'Elsae' plus 'Clyne Blush' and 'Clyne Cerise'. 'Clyne Elsae' has fuchsia-purple flowers, more richly coloured at the margins, all named after Clyne Castle near Swansea in Wales, Heneage-Vivian's former home. It is now home to national collections of both the Falconera and Grande sections.

'Fortune'

R. falconeri ssp. *falconeri* x *R. sinograde*

Raised and registered by Lionel de Rothschild, from Exbury Gardens, Hampshire, England before 1938. It's a very handsome plant with large dense heads of pale yellow flowers each with a crimson central blotch. The leaves favour the female parent, having long large leaves with a matt finish. This is the original clone of the 'Fortune' grex.

First Class Certificate, 1938

R. 'Fortune'.

'Geoff Broker'

Grown from seed sent from the USA to New Zealand as *R. protistum*. It's definitely part *R. macabeanum* but with foliage that is closer to *R. protistum*. Has very large peachy trusses that pale to cream-yellow flowers and bold elliptic leaves up to 16 in (40 cm) long with thin grey indumentum. Geoff Broker was the first secretary of Pukeiti Rhododendron Trust. The hybrid was named by Graham Smith.

'Glenshant'

R. grande x *R. macabeanum*

Big bold leaves with silver indumentum. This Brodick Castle hybrid has creamy-white flowers with a hint of yellow, providing a true mix of the parents.

Award of Merit, 1964

'Golden Dawn'

R. macabeanum x unknown

A George Huthnance, New Zealand seedling worth growing for the gorgeous golden-yellow trumpets. Excellent foliage of a typical big-leaf but the plant is of modest proportions and suitable for smaller gardens. One of the best hybrids for gardens but unfortunately it has not been distributed much. George Huthnance took to collecting seed off rhododendrons he liked the look of regardless of parentage, and grew on and selected many from hundreds of seedlings in New Zealand. Names such as 'Elaine Rowe', 'Mrs George Huthnance', 'Eyestopper', 'Pink Frills', 'Jean Church', and 'Les Boisen' have all been distributed in New Zealand.

'Gordon Collier'

R. protistum 'Pukeiti' x *R. magnificum*

A chance seedling found at Pukeiti gardens in New Zealand. The parentage is almost certainly *R. protistum* 'Pukeiti' x *R. magnificum* resulting in the very large cerise flowers typical of the cross with bold leaves to match, glabrous early and developing thin fawn indumentum later. Selected and named by Graham Smith.

R. 'Geoff Broker' (top), *R.* 'Golden Dawn' (middle) and *R.* 'Gordon Collier' (bottom).

'Grand Prix'

R. grande x *R. falconeri* ssp. *eximium*

White or off-white flowers with a hint of red. Raised and named by Heneage-Vivian of Clyne Castle near Swansea, Wales.

Award of Merit RHS, 1940

'Grandex'

R. falconeri ssp. *eximium* x *R. sinogrande*

Yellow flowers with a hint of pink. Bred by Lord Aberconway, and registered in 1950.

'Haze'

R. hodgsonii x *R.* 'Muriel' (*R. falconeri* ssp. *falconeri* x *R. grande*)

Raised by Sir Giles Loder of Leonardslee Garden in Sussex and registered in 1954. The flowers are pink to mauve. Part of the grex 'Evening' which also includes the clone 'Mist'.

'Himalayan Child'

R. hodgsonii x *R. falconeri* ssp. *falconeri*

Thought to be a naturally occurring hybrid. Collected as wild seed by Frank Kingdon Ward, KW 13681, as a possible *R. sinogrande*. An open, loose truss of purple flowers with a darker throat. Silver-brown indumentum on a big bold leaf. Raised and registered by the Royal Gardens, Windsor.

'Ina Hair'

Named after the wife of Rob Hair, the third Pukeiti curator. A *macabeanum* type George Huthnance seedling, relatively low and compact with multi-layered leaves. This compact nature and attractive dense, silver-backed foliage make it a contender for smaller gardens. Flowers are soft pink in bud opening to creamy-yellow with a small dark eye, floriferous from a young age and flowering in March to April and September to October in the southern hemisphere

R. grande hybrid, at Olinda, Australia (top), and *R.* 'Ina Hair' (bottom).

'Jack Anderson'

R. magnificum x *R. macabeanum*

Named after the charismatic second secretary of Pukeiti 1961–1985 from a batch of seedlings after twenty years from sowing. The cross was made at Pukeiti by Graham Smith to see if it produced offspring similar to many plants growing there from early Scottish seed. Most are cream to blush flowers with a dark eye but this clone has rich pink flowers with a yellowish tube giving a bi-colour effect. Leaves are dark green with a thin grey indumentum below.

'James Deans'

R. griersonianum x *R. grande*

Bred by Les Jury, New Zealand, this is a medium-sized shrub with large attractive foliage, grey indumentum below and large reddish flower trusses quickly paling to light pink. It flowers at a young age. Similar hybrids from the same cross are 'Les Jury' and 'New Plymouth City', all with similar colouring.

'Joy Bells'

R. macabeanum x *R.* 'Fortune' *(R. falconeri* ssp. *falconeri* x *R. sinogrande)*

A New Zealand hybrid with creamy champagne colours and a red internal blotch. The best thing about it is the compact size making it suitable for smaller gardens and its tendency to flower from an early age. Bred by Joseph Joyce. The cultivar 'Joyce' is from the same cross.

'Koenig Carola'

R. falconeri x *R. ponticum*

An interesting cross and quite attractive, but not really looking like a large-leaf, though the foliage is good. The flowers are pale lavender, more intense on the tips of the corolla and having a spotty throat. It shows what can be done with crossing outside the Section, in a similar way to 'Spiced Honey'. It's an old Scandinavian hybrid raised by Ludiecke in 1926.

R. 'Jack Anderson' (top), *R.* 'Joy Bells' (middle) and *R.* 'Koenig Carola' (bottom).

'Little Jessica'

R. hodgsonii x unknown

Raised at the Reuthe Nursery by J.T. Boscawen in 1914, but only registered in 1989 so has survived a long time without recognition.

'Loch Awe'

'Percy Wiseman' x *R. macabeanum*

A Glendoick cross from Perth, Scotland obviously aimed at producing a compact, hardy, smaller-garden hybrid. The pale yellow flowers are suffused with peach with red spotting. Large handsome leaves with thin indumentum below.

'Mecca'

R. falconeri ssp. *falconeri* x *R. niveum*

A very dense head with forty or more flowers. Basically white flowers have a hint of purple and a deep red blotch within.
Bred by Mrs Dale Gordon in the United Kingdom it is the same cross as 'Colonel Rodgers'.

Award of Merit, RHS, 1965

'Michael Beekman'

R. macabeanum x unknown

An Australian hybrid raised by J. Beekman and part of a grex all named after family members. The flowers are a very unusual colour being red on opening and gradually fading to yellow. Good truss size with up to twenty flowers in a head.

'Middlemarch'

R. sinograhde x *R. lacteum*

Bred by Colonel S.R. Clarke at Borde Hill Gardens, West Sussex. The heads are very dense and open pure white with an intense red blotch in the throat.

Award of Merit, RHS, 1980

'Milton Hollard'

R. macabeanum x unknown

Usually twenty-two flowers in a truss, opening pink and then quickly fading to pale yellow with a hint of pink. The flowers have a red spotty throat. A wide-spreading small tree with elliptic leaves, silver-grey below. Raised and registered in New Zealand by Bernard Hollard in 1979 and named after his son.

'Mist'

R. hodgsonii x 'Muriel' (R. falconeri ssp. falconeri x R. grande)

A clever idea to combine the genes of the three well-known giant rhododendrons. The flowers are a rich pinky-mauve. R. 'Evening' and R. 'Haze' are part of the same grex. Bred and registered by Sir Giles Loder, 1954.

'Mrs Henry Agnew'

R. grande x R. arboreum var. album

Raised in Cornwall by J.H. Mangles in 1915, this is eventually a tall-growing tree with white flowers fringed with pink.

'Muriel'

R. falconeri ssp. falconeri x R. grande

Bred and registered by Sir Edmund Loder (son of Sir Giles), Horsham, Sussex, England, 1925. This same cross was done fifty years before resulting in 'Mansellii' when shown by John Downie.

A very elegant plant decked in pure white flowers with a tiny central blotch of red wine. The leaves are handsome with a dull rugose surface and hirsute below; the indumentum is pale brown.

'My Delight'

R. macabeanum x R. macabeanum

Raised at Brodick Castle in Scotland, this plant is a cross between two good clones of R. macabeanum so not really a hybrid. Over the years, several breeders have employed this trick of crossing two good forms of one species to create a batch of top-notch seedlings. In this case the flowers are a pale creamy-yellow, but the leaves are good.

'Our Kate'

R. calophytum x R. macabeanum

A charming pink rhododendron with a loose truss and flowers in two shades of pale pink. A deep rich-red inner throat. Named by Lionel de Rothschild for his eldest daughter.

Award of Merit, 1963

'Pacific Rim'

'Loderi King George' x R. macabeanum

This hybrid manages to capture the pink of the 'Loderi' and some of the bold R. macabeanum leaf. Raised in 1950 and registered by Hjalmar L. Larson in 1982, in Washington State, USA.

'Powder Snow'

R. degronianum ssp. *yakushimanum* Exbury form x *R. macabeanum*

Jim Barlup of Bellevue, Washington State, USA, has seemingly created the perfect big-leaf for small gardens. By using *R. yakushimanum*, the highest quality female parent, he has managed to keep the plant small while also incorporating the rugose leaf of *R. macabeanum*. The underside of each leaf is very hirsute.

The flowers are pure white with a tiny red blotch in the top centre interior. The heads are quite dense with up to twenty flowers and are not unlike other *R. yakushimanum* hybrids such as 'Coconut Ice'. But what he has captured is a biggish rugose leaf on a compact, hardy plant. If you saw the plant without any flowers you would think it was a typical big-leaf type. The *R. yakushimanum* blood gives it the hardiness, making it possible for many more gardeners around the world to grow it. A sister seedling named 'Laramie' has ivory-white flowers. The leaves are shinier but still favouring the *R. macabeanum* in appearance. It has a similar dwarf, dense habit suitable for small gardens.

'Ronald'

R. hodgsonii x *R. sinogrande*

Bred by the Gibson brothers at Glenarn, Rhu, in Scotland in 1933. It has up to thirty white suffused with rose-purple flowers packed in a big flower head and heavy, bold, dark-green foliage.

Award of Merit, 1958

'Spiced Honey'

R. macabeanum x 'Unique'

Raised by the New Zealand Rhododendron Association, seedlings were distributed to members in the late 1960s. This selection was from Lachie Grant's Timaru garden and has pink buds opening amber with a red blotch, gradually paling to cream. Foliage is like a smaller *R. macabeanum*. A good dense habit makes it an ideal shrub for the smaller garden.

R. 'Spiced Honey'.

'Surprise'

R. falconeri x *R. thomsonii*

First raised by J. Waterer in Surrey before 1867 and was said to be mauve with a black blotch. 'Surprise Packet', the same cross, was registered by Lord Digby, of Minterne House and Gardens in Dorset, in 1953 and another called 'Faltho' by Loder which received an Award of Merit in 1954. This one is rose-madder with faint spotting and a crimson blotch.

'Thoron Hollard'

R. macabeanum x unknown

Very pink buds fade to creamy-white. A strong red throat in the centre of the flower lights up the bloom. It's a small tree, raised and registered by Bernard Hollard (Hollard Gardens, Taranaki) in 1979 and named after his son Thoron, a sister-seedling of 'Milton Hollard'.

R. wardii x *R. macabeanum*

A new hybrid from the Cox stable at Glendoick, Scotland, with large yellow trusses, red blotched, and handsome big leaves. It should be hardier than the large-leaf parent *R. macabeanum* as the *R. wardii* should impart some hardiness.

R. 'Thoron Hollard'.

"Whidbey Island'

R. niveum x *R. rex* ssp. *rex*

Raised by A. Meerkerk (Meerkerk Gardens, Washington State, USA) in 1977 this has fine rich purple-pink trusses with a crimson blotch paling to light mauve with a white tube. The leaves are dark green, oblanceolate with grey woolly indumentum below. A large shrub suitable for woodland conditions.

'White Dane'

R. yakushimanum x *R. galactinum*

This rather striking cultivar is a hybrid between a big-leaf and a dwarf *R. yakushimanum* type, *R. degronianum* ssp. *yakushimanum*. Bred by Jens Birk in Denmark for colder-climate reliability, it looks for all the world like a Yak hybrid, being a dense, compact shrub with smooth, curved leaves, somewhat larger than its seed parent. The flowers are pure white and it covers itself with good-sized trusses.

CHAPTER 7

Where to find them — rhododendron gardens around the world

Naturally these plants are suited to moist forests and they are quite happy in their Himalayan homeland. For gardeners the challenge is to attempt to imitate these high-altitude, high-rainfall conditions. Without a doubt, maritime climates are the best. The ideal places are mild regions with a prevailing onshore wind bringing regular rain throughout the year. Gardens at higher altitude have the added advantage of cooler temperatures, and more frequent rainfall. The other key is acidic soil because rhododendrons, in cultivation, hate limestone country.

The west coast of Britain, with the warmer currents of the Gulf Stream coming up from Mexico, has traditionally been thought of as the perfect climate for rhododendrons and especially for the big-leaf versions. South-west Ireland, Cornwall, west and south Wales and western Scotland are all blessed with warm wet climates ideal for rhododendrons.

Likewise the onshore winds bringing regular rain and cool temperatures to northern California, Oregon and Vancouver make for excellent rhododendron country. The soils and moist climate are perfect for them.

Parts of southern Australia especially around Melbourne are cool and moist enough to grow rhododendrons well; Tasmania, with its constant rain-bearing winds, is even better.

Those same dominant westerlies also find their way to the west coast of New Zealand. The south of the South Island and all up the west coast of both islands is good rhododendron country. Some areas in the east of the country manage to grow them well despite the frequent droughts.

Opposite: Stonefield Castle, Scotland, with *R. falconeri*.

GARDENS IN CANADA AND THE USA

UNIVERSITY OF BRITISH COLUMBIA BOTANICAL GARDEN

6804 SW Marine Drive, Vancouver, British Columbia, Canada

www.botanicalgarden.ubc.ca

Founded in 1916 by a Scottish botanist, John Davidson (1878–1970). As Provincial Botanist his role was to record the local flora using herbarium specimens and to create a live collection where feasible. In 1916, his twin collections were relocated from Essendale, 60 km from the University of British Columbia, Vancouver. A team of volunteers cleared the land and began planting more than 25,000 plants. The efforts of those determined people paid off and now the garden is well established. Despite two world wars and numerous funding problems the garden has survived due in large part to John Davidson.

The gardens fulfil a multi-purpose role for teaching, research and also conservation, especially of rare Asian plants.

The UBC garden rhododendron collection took on much greater importance after new material from Britain was imported in the 1960s. The moist maritime climate provides excellent growing conditions for rhododendrons. With the arrival of the late Peter Wharton (1950–2008) from Britain in the mid '70s, the garden developed at a great pace and is now at the forefront of the rhododendron scene thanks to Peter's efforts.

With his cooperative style and network of plant people around the world, he acquired a phenomenal collection which put the Asian garden on the map and the collection took on world status. Many of the plants he collected himself, travelling to China, Korea and Taiwan to gather seed. These new collections are now in the David C. Lam Asian Garden and include many large-leaf rhododendrons.

THE RHODODENDRON SPECIES BOTANICAL GARDEN

2525 S 336th St, Federal Way, WA 98003, United States

www.rhodygarden.org

The Rhododendron Species Foundation (RSF) in Washington State, western USA, describes itself as 'a non-profit organization dedicated to the conservation, research, acquisition, evaluation, cultivation, public display and distribution of rhododendron species'.

The Foundation does a wonderful job of promoting and educating people about rhododendrons through their very informative website, and in the real world with a fine species garden in the grounds of the Weyerhaeuser Company in Federal Way just south of Seattle, Washington. The company generously leases the site at no charge. Covering 24 acres (10 hectares), this site was planted in taxonomic grouping in 1974/5. Prior to that, the collection was housed in two private gardens: firstly in Dr Milton Walker's property in Pleasant Hill, Eugene, Oregon, and then later in P.H. (Jock) Brydon's garden near Salem, Oregon.

The collection was instigated by Dr Walker in 1964 when he visited Britain with the express purpose of importing cuttings of the best forms of rhododendron species. Britain was seen as the home of rhododendrons since most of the early seed gatherers were British. The gardens all agreed to send plant material but there was a hitch — American import regulations would not allow material from Britain to enter the country. By chance the US would allow material in from Canada and so a scheme was hatched whereby the material went from Britain to Mary Grieg at the Royston Nursery on Vancouver Island and subsequently crossed the border to Oregon. The University of British Columbia was also given an identical set of plants.

The Rhododendron Species Botanical Garden is now regarded as a living plant museum and plays a key role in identification, research and education. The garden has one of the largest collections of species rhododendrons in the world with over 600 of an estimated 1000 species thought to exist in the wild. One of their major missions is conservation, both at home and abroad. They do this by adding to the collection using material sourced from the wild and also by encouraging conservation in the homelands of the rhododendrons. A large Vireya collection is housed in the new Rutherford Conservatory.

The RSF has a strong public membership. Some of these enthusiasts and staff members have collected rhododendron seed in the wilds of Asia and North America. The garden is doubly blessed to have Steve Hootman as their Director and Curator. As plant experts go, he's the best.

Meerkerk Rhododendron Gardens, Washington State, US.

MEERKERK RHODODENDRON GARDENS

3531 Meerkerk Lane, Greenbank, WA 98253, United States

www.meerkerkgardens.org

Meerkerk Rhododendron Gardens is the result of the foresight and enterprise of Ann and Max Meerkerk. Between them they created a 53-acre (22-hectare) garden on Whidbey Island on Puget Sound, just north of Seattle. They began this project in the early 1960s, inspired by the famous British woodland gardens. They wanted to create a haven for natural wildlife and for plants, especially rhododendrons.

There is a strong emphasis on hybrid rhododendrons and they do lot of breeding on site. The species or wild rhododendron are not neglected, though, and in this perfect climate they have established a 'Big-Leaf Valley', home to dozens of rare big-leaf *grande*-type rhododendrons under a Douglas fir canopy.

The area is perfect for rhododendron with acid-free, draining soils and frequent rainfall from the constant westerlies. When Ann Meerkerk died in 1979, she bequeathed the gardens to the Seattle Rhododendron Society. Now it is run on a not-for-profit basis with the preservation and improvement of rhododendrons as the paramount objective. The garden is run by volunteers and open to the public during flowering season.

A hybrid 'test garden' is an ever-changing display of the latest varieties from USA breeders.

SCOTLAND

Note: The Scottish gardens are listed in sequence starting with Brodick Castle on the Isle of Arran to the west of Glasgow and then back to the mainland heading north to Glenarn.

BRODICK CASTLE GARDEN

Isle of Arran, North Ayrshire, KA27 8HY

R. sinogrande dell in the garden at Brodick Castle, Scotland.

Brodick is a fascinating property with a long history. There has been a castle on this site since the thirteenth century, though the current castle was built in the late 1500s. Belonging to the Hamilton family for over 500 years, it passed in name to the Montrose family in 1906 when the Sixth Duke of Montrose married Mary the only daughter of the Twelfth Duke of Hamilton. In 1957 it was given to the National Trust for Scotland to avoid death duties.

Rhododendron montroseanum previously called *R. mollyanum* was both times named after Mary, Molly being her pet family name, but this species name could not be kept as there is a similarly named tropical rhododendron. It's very appropriate this splendid species should be named after someone so dedicated to the genus.

It was during the Montrose era, from 1906 onwards, that the

gardens were restored using new material from outside sources, including seed collected in Yunnan by George Forrest. During this time the focus was on new plants from the Himalayas, especially rhododendrons, primulas and alpines. The property has a massive 75 acres (30 hectares) of woodland garden with extensive collections of rhododendrons and boasts one of the best congregations of big-leaf species rhododendrons anywhere in the world.

Understandably the garden holds the British 'national collection' for the rhododendron Grandia and Falconera series (Swansea also holds one for the Falconera series). 'National' collections are exactly that — the best collection in the country. The garden is also home to the Gigha collection of rhododendron hybrids which were donated to Brodick in the early 1970s.

Brodick is ideally suited to growing big-leaf rhododendron because it has a mild, moist climate fed by the constant Gulf Stream flow of warm water and the predominant south-westerly winds. Although the Isle of Arran is 1000 miles north of New York, the Gulf Stream nevertheless guarantees a milder climate than its latitude would suggest. Rain falls throughout the year to give an average rainfall of 70 in (1.8 m). It rarely snows and frosts are generally limited from January to March and so late frosts, the cause of so many problems for others, are quite rare here. Besides the warm winters averaging 10°C (50°F), another aspect favouring rhododendron cultivation is the cool summers where temperatures rarely go above 20°C (70°F).

The soil is a sandy loam with lots of nourishing leaf litter on a bedrock of sandstone. The rhododendrons are mostly on south-facing slopes under deciduous trees and conifers. The mild winters allow the rhododendrons to thrive and in the case of the very early flowers on *R. protistum giganteum* and *R. magnificum*, to display their best rather than being killed by frost as happens in so many gardens.

The fame of Brodick was enhanced by the massive exhibition of cut flowers sent to the London Royal Horticultural Society (RHS) fortnightly shows by the head gardener, John Basford. John would pick the blooms, pack them in damp moss and paper in a van, catch the ferry and drive to London all in twenty-four hours. The displays were legendary and many rhododendrons received RHS Awards through these exhibits.

GLENARN

Glenarn Road, Rhu, Helensburgh, G84 8LL

www.gardens-of-argyll.co.uk/gardens/glenarn

Glenarn is a wonderful private garden to the north-west of Glasgow in Rhu, north of Helensburgh. Unlike so many of the Scottish gardens it has natural protection from the strong south-west winds because it lies in a dell. But those constant southwesters do bring the warm air and ocean currents of the Gulf Stream, allowing gardeners in this region to grow exotic subtropical plants. The house was built in the 1830s. The owners were friends of Joseph Hooker and received both seeds and plants of Himalayan rhododendrons from him. Some of these early 1850s collections, the first examples in cultivation, still exist.

The property was bought by the Gibson family in 1927 and new collections established using seed from Kingdon Ward and later from Ludlow and Sherriff. George Sherriff was a family friend and among other things, gave them a delightful soft-pink form of *R. griffithianum*, L & S 2835.

The garden is rightly famous for these rhododendron collections, including many of the big-leaf or tree types. The garden is also sheltered enough to be host to a variety of magnolias. In 1983, the Thornley family acquired Glenarn and immediately began renovating the tired parts of the garden.

ROYAL BOTANIC GARDEN, EDINBURGH

Arboretum Place, Edinburgh EH3 5NZ

And including Benmore Botanic Garden, Argyll, Benmore, Dunoon PA23 8QU

www.rbge.org.uk

These gardens are justly famous for rhododendrons. With the likes of George Forrest, Isaac Bayley Balfour, William Wright Smith, H.H. Davidian and David Chamberlain all associated with the garden, it plays a major part in the history of rhododendrons. Nowadays, Edinburgh boasts the best collection of rhododendrons in the world, albeit in four locations to get the benefit of four different climates. From our perspective of big-leaf rhododendrons, their Benmore site just west of Loch Lomond north of Glasgow is the prime focus.

Benmore is set in Loch Lomond and the Trossachs National Park. The garden is the perfect mountain habitat for big-leaf rhododendrons with its high rainfall and mild conditions. Previously a private estate, the idea of a west coast outpost for Edinburgh came from Isaac Bayley Balfour. In times past the estate belonged to rich American Piers Patrick, who bought it in 1863 and who is responsible for the avenue of giant sequoiadendrons — an inspirational choice.

A few years later it passed to James Duncan, a wealthy sugar merchant who organised the planting of literally millions of conifers on the estate. The estate belonged to the Younger family, from 1889, and the diversity of planting increased. Harry Younger gifted the garden to the nation in 1925 and a few years later it became part of the Edinburgh Botanics.

Nowadays, the garden has fabulous collections, especially of the floras of Bhutan, Chile, Japan and Tasmania. It's the Bhutan section which interests rhododendron enthusiasts as it's the home of many choice species including *R. kesangiae* and *R. griffithianum*.

The garden is world famous for its conifers and rhododendron. The conifers are recognised as a National Pinetum with many rare and tender conifers added in recent times. With around 300 rhododendron species and subspecies it's a Mecca for rhodophiles.

Edinburgh Botanics is at the forefront of rhododendron research and have continuing strong ties with rhododendron-rich countries, such as Bhutan and China.

ARDKINGLAS WOODLAND GARDEN

The Estate Office, Ardkinglas Estate, Cairndow, Argyll & Bute PA26 8BG

www.ardkinglas.com

This lovely old garden is at the top of Loch Fyne in the village of Cairndow north of Inveraray. The name comes from the nearby Kinglas River. Famous for its fabulous old trees and collections of rhododendrons, this is a must-visit garden for any serious rhodophile. The garden has been here for centuries but was turned into a serious conifer collection sometime in the 1830s by the Laird of Ardkinglas, James Henry Callander. At the time, new conifers were being discovered by the score by Scottish collector David Douglas. Ardkinglas now boasts some truly magnificent trees including several champion trees.

This conifer collection formed the basis of the garden developed by the new owners, the Noble family, beginning in 1905 with Sir Andrew Noble. During the next two decades many newly introduced rhododendrons were planted and included many of the big-leaf types. Grandson Michael Noble married Lady Anne Glenkinglas and together they enhanced the collection of rhododendrons and also widened the scope of the garden to include more variation and beauty.

They built a new house and developed the garden around it, changing the name to Strone Woodland Garden for many years before parts of the estate were sold, and then the garden was bought back by the family to continue the tradition of gardening here beside the loch.

Lovers of big-leaf rhododendrons will be impressed with the ancient *R. falconeri* and other giant species planted back in the early 1900s.

Ardkinglas Woodland Garden, Scotland.

CRARAE GARDEN

Minard, Inveraray, Argyll, PA32 8YA

www.nts.org.uk/property/crarae-garden

Imagine a Himalayan valley magically transported to western Scotland; this is Crarae on the banks of Loch Fyne, ten miles (16 km) south of Inveraray on the A83. It's a large 50-acre (20-hectare) garden created in a rocky gorge where the Crarae burn or stream tumbles down to the loch. The overall property is more than twice this size. The garden is famous for its bridges, giving unusual angles and aspects of plants, and also for the views out of the garden across the loch.

It was developed by three generations of Campbells, beginning with Lady Grace Campbell in 1912. In an era of new plants and new ideas she began the process of creating a garden. Plants and gardening were in the blood as she was the aunt of Reginald Farrer, the famous plant collector and rockery doyen. In 1925, her son Sir George Campbell took over and created what we see today — a fantastic collection of Himalayan and southern hemisphere trees and shrubs.

They hold the National Collection of southern hemisphere beeches or *Nothofagus*.

Sir George's son, Sir Ilay Campbell, inherited the garden in 1967 and more recently it was saved by the National Trust for Scotland after a fund-raising appeal in 2001. The Trust is enhancing the collection as well as replacing and restoring the infrastructure such as bridges and steps.

The garden is home to many rhododendrons including a large collection of Falconera and Grandia types. Many of these were collected in the wild and so are doubly valuable. The group of aged *R. falconeri* with their twisting sinuous trunks will take your breath away. These were apparently planted way back in 1912 by Grace Campbell. In recent times, the gardeners have been updating and planting recent wild-collected plants from both sections.

STONEFIELD CASTLE

Stonefield, Tarbert, Loch Fyne, Argyll, PA29 6YJ

On the east side of the Kintyre Peninsula near the village of Tarbert, this fairy-tale castle was built as recently as 1837. This remarkable building is so stunning it's easy to forget we're here to look at rhododendrons. The consolation is the castle is now a hotel so you can stay here and imagine yourself the Laird during the evening, while studying rhododendrons by day.

Extensive gardens and woodland walks cover 60 acres (25 hectares), for you to stroll and enjoy. Not only do they have a fine collection of big-leaf rhododendrons, but they have some of the originals in cultivation. The Campbells, the original owners, were friends of Sir William Hooker, Professor of Botany in Glasgow. His son Joseph Hooker discovered the first Himalayan rhododendron in the early 1850s. Hooker's travelling companion, Dr Archibald Campbell, Political Resident in Sikkim, sent seeds back to Scotland, including to the Campbells (no relation) at Stonefield.

Among other fine plants, the garden contains the first *R. grande* in cultivation and collected in Sikkim by Hooker.

Crarae Garden (top, left) and *R. arboreum* and *falconeri* at Stonefield Castle (bottom, left) Scotland.

ACHAMORE GARDENS

Isle of Gigha Heritage Trust, Craft Workshops, Isle of Gigha, Argyll, PA41 7AA

www.gigha.org.uk/gardens

These gardens are remarkable for several reasons, including their location, climate and history. They are situated on the Isle of Gigha which lies just a few miles west of the famous Kintyre Peninsula, and directly west of Glasgow. As of March 2002, the island belongs to the inhabitants and so the garden is community-owned and administered by a Heritage Trust.

Achamore Gardens, Scotland.

The fabulous mansion, Achamore House, was built in 1884 by Captain James Scarlett, the Third Lord Abinger. He not only built the house, but was responsible for the planting of the older shelter trees. It was he who saw the worth of the screens of trees to protect the garden from the severe salt-laden gales. What is now a sheltered microclimate would be a salt-blasted heath without his foresight.

Sir James Horlick bought the estate in 1944. His passion was rhododendrons and luckily the combination of local climate and existing shelter allowed them to thrive. The island receives the benefit of the Gulf Stream and the consequent mild climate allows them to grow many subtropical plants from the southern hemisphere. As you might imagine, frosts and snow are thankfully uncommon. The rainfall is low, around 40–50 in (1–1.25 m) but the kindness of the climate compensates. Most of the garden is an acid sandy loam with a free-draining gravel subsoil.

The garden he created is an impressive display covering 55 acres (20 hectares). Horlick died in 1971 but left a fabulous collection including a wide range of rhododendron species as well as hybrids, many of which he bred himself.

If you wish to enjoy the gardens, it's possible to stay in Achamore House as it is now a bed and breakfast establishment. The garden is being revamped by the head gardener, Micky Little. Rhododendrons are propagated to ensure continuity and many of the older plants have been cut back to reinvigorate them. New exciting plants such as tree ferns have been added to create drama and excitement.

ARDUAINE GARDEN

Arduaine, Oban, Argyll & Bute PA34 4XQ

www.nts.org.uk/arduainegarden

To the north-west of Glasgow and heading towards Oban along the coast you'll find Arduaine Garden, or rather you'll find the Loch Melfort Hotel. Park your car here and wander down to this delightful garden. Blessed with a mild climate thanks to the ever-present Gulf Stream, a garden was created and developed by three generations of Campbells, from 1898 onwards. They were all inspired by Osgood Mackenzie at Inverewe who gave advice on planting.

In 1971, the gardens were purchased by two brothers from Essex. The Wright brothers, Edmund and Harry, revamped the garden and then gave it to the National Trust for Scotland in 1992 for all to enjoy.

It's a wet garden for a wet climate and described as 'moist and mossy'. There are ponds, aquatic plants and some very happy rhododendrons as well as southern hemisphere plants which relish the regular rainfall. The garden is blessed with dazzling azaleas, camellias and early magnolias, and a surprising range of perennials. In the way that gardeners do, the Campbells acquired some of the big-leaf rhododendrons from other Scottish gardens.

They have a superb *R. protistum* and *R. falconeri* as well as *R. sinogrande*, *R. giganteum* and a fine *R. auriculatum*.

INVEREWE GARDENS

Poolewe, Achnasheen IV22 2LG

www.nts.org.uk/Property/Inverewe-Garden-and-Estate

Inverewe Gardens are on the shore of Loch Ewe on the west coast of Scotland up in the highlands. Nestled on a hillside on the north-eastern edge of Loch Ewe, the view from this property is sublime, never mind the gardens. The dominant Gulf Stream keeps this place warm in winter and cool in summer. It's almost the perfect climate for people and plants, where frosts are rare, as are sweltering days during summer.

Inverewe Gardens, Scotland.

The garden is famous for tender exotics like New Zealand daisy bushes and Australian gum trees. Equally impressive are the rhododendrons in spring and it is home to an amazing collection of big-leaf rhododendrons. The garden was the brainchild of local man Osgood Mackenzie. Born in 1842, the son of a local laird, his brother inherited the estate so he bought this property and set about building a fabulous home on the shores of the loch. While the climate is kind in terms of temperature, the region is prone to strong salt-laden winds and so he set about planting shelter trees. He chose the reliable native *Pinus sylvestris* and today the garden enjoys sheltered views over the loch.

When he died in 1922, his daughter Mairi ran the garden until her death in 1953. Fortunately she bequeathed the property to the National Trust for Scotland before she died and it is now available for all to see.

ENGLAND AND WALES

MUNCASTER CASTLE

Ravenglass, Cumbria CA18 1RQ

www.muncaster.co.uk/

Situated near the coast west of the Lake District in the north-west of England, the castle has been in the same family for over 800 years. The garden part of the estate covers nearly 80 acres (32 hectares) and provides astonishing views towards the sea.

Lord Muncaster began planting the site with trees in the 1780s to give shelter from the strong westerly winds. The site is open to the west and while it enjoys the frequent rains, the gales can be tiresome. But the warm Gulf Stream is a blessing, allowing many tender plants to be grown here.

With the shelter these trees provided and the acid soil, it was the perfect site for Sir John Ramsden, the Sixth Baronet, to create a fantastic collection of rhododendrons, culminating in what was considered the best collection of wild species in Europe at that time. He subscribed to expeditions by Kingdon Ward and also Ludlow and Sherriff, further enhancing his fine collection.

Sir John's grandchildren and their team are trying to recreate those glory days by planting new shelter trees and enhancing the collection of rhododendrons with modern wild collections, especially from Alan Clark who was curator of the gardens until 2000.

BODNANT GARDEN

Bodnant Road
Tal-y-Cafn, Conwy LL28 5RE, Wales

www.bodnant-estate.co.uk/bodnant-garden

Bodnant has been described as a 'masterpiece' and as 'the best garden in Britain'. In many ways it is perfection, with beauty, colour and a feeling of everything in its place. It's an architectural delight with vast sweeping lawns, clever ornamentation, water features and smooth plant transitions. Certainly the general public regard it as gardening as it should be. And while all those things are true, the real plants-person looks beyond the 'pretties' and is entranced by the connoisseur plants. The combination of rare maples, birches, magnolias and rhododendrons is definitely worth a visit. Many are planted in a deep ravine with a river running through, imitating the natural environment of their homeland.

Bodnant Garden, Wales.

With good acid soil and a mild and moist climate, it's ideally suited to growing all these treasures. The house was built in 1792 and many of the trees were planted around this time. Then in 1874 Henry Pochin bought the estate and it was later inherited by his daughter Laura and her husband Charles McLaren, First Lord Aberconway. An industrialist with a passion for plants he set about creating a garden. In the early 1900s, he subscribed to various plant-hunting trips and became especially keen on rhododendrons.

Henry the Second Lord Aberconway and Charles the Third, both continued this fine tradition, ably assisted by three generations of head gardeners. Frederick Puddle became head gardener in 1920 followed by his son Charles Puddle in 1947 and grandson Martin in 1982.

SAVILL GARDEN (WINDSOR GREAT PARK)

Englefield Green, Nr. Windsor, TW20 0UU

www.theroyallandscape.co.uk/gardens-and-landscape/the-savill-garden/

In 1932, King George VI and Queen Elizabeth enlisted the help of Sir Eric Savill to create a new garden within Windsor Great Park using a previously unused piece of land. The main part of this garden, now known as the Savill Garden, is 35 acres (15 hectares). Another huge woodland area was later developed by Sir Eric Savill and is known as the Valley Garden. Both areas have a fantastic collection of rare and wondrous trees including magnolias, unusual oaks, maples and pines. The garden is justly famous for its rhododendrons, especially the masses of blooming hybrids in the spring. For the connoisseur rhodophile there is a magnificent collection of big-leaf and tree rhododendrons. The acid soil and sheltered environment might seem perfect but the low rainfall and dry atmosphere is not ideal for Himalayan rhododendrons. However, to see the healthy specimens here you would not imagine the climate is a hindrance. A combination of good setting, adequate mulching and irrigation seem to overcome any problems the climate might engender.

Springtime at the Savill Garden, Windsor Great Park, England.

For the casual visitor it's a pleasant garden ramble with a beautiful central lake and a very interesting array of trees, shrubs and herbaceous plants. The Valley Gardens to the north of Virginia Water are more natural and seem like a woodland ramble but are host to many rare plants. The rhododendron collection was greatly enhanced in the early 1940s by Sir Eric Savill's connections with the Magor family, owners of the Lamellen garden near St Tudy in Cornwall.

Edward Magor grew rhododendron seedlings collected by E.H. Wilson for Veitch Nurseries in 1899–1902 and again in 1903–1905. Having been bitten by the bug, he also received seed from plant-hunting expeditions by Reginald Farrer, George Forrest, Joseph Rock, and Frank Kingdon Ward between 1909 and 1925.

As gardeners do, he swapped plants with J.C. Williams of Caerhays Castle and others to develop one of the best collections in the country. Near the end of his days and with growing concern for his precious rhododendron collection, Edward Magor donated much of it to Sir Eric Savill to be planted in the Savill and Valley Gardens, Windsor.

Another species collection came from J.B. Stevenson's garden at nearby Tower Court, in the 1940s, after his death. It took two years to lift and transport the many mature specimens to the Valley Garden.

EXBURY GARDENS

Exbury Estate Office, Exbury, Summer Lane, Exbury, Southampton SO45 1AZ

www.exbury.co.uk/

Directly south of Southampton on the south coast of England, this fabulous garden nestles near the sea in the famous New Forest. It's a perfect spot, overlooking the Solent and out to the Isle of Wight. Exbury covers 200 acres (80 hectares) and is an incredible informal woodland garden, dominated by rhododendrons.

Exbury Gardens as they are today were created by Lionel de Rothschild who bought the property in 1919. A banker by profession, his obsession was rhododendrons and he and his son Edmund went on to create one of the best collections of rhododendrons in the world.

Exbury Gardens, England.

It is not a particularly good climate for rhodos as the rainfall is a low 24 in (610 mm) but an artificial water supply installed by Lionel overcame those problems. On the plus side, the garden is warm by English standards and can sometimes enjoy frost-free winters. The soil, too, is rather poor, being a gravel loam, but it's ideally suited to rhododendrons as it is acid in nature.

From 1919 until his death in 1942 Lionel pursued his passion, acquiring as many hybrid and species rhododendrons as possible and even breeding them. The 'Naomi' grex of hybrids and many others grace our gardens today. Over the years more fine hybrids have emerged from Exbury including some stunning reds such as 'Leo' and 'Edmund de Rothschild', and clear yellows such as the 'Hawk' grex.

Lionel de Rothschild contributed funds to George Forrest and Kingdon Ward for their efforts to collect new species of rhododendron. Naturally Exbury built up one of the best collections of wild species including the magnificent Falconera and Grandia types. Lionel began using these giants for hybridising culminating, in the wonderful 'Fortune' grex (*R. falconeri* x *R. sinogrande*). The garden is still owned and progressed by the family, each generation adding to the overall picture.

ABBOTSBURY SUBTROPICAL GARDENS

Bullers Way, Abbotsbury, Nr Weymouth, Dorset DT3 4LA

www.abbotsbury-tourism.co.uk/gardens

Dorchester is the county town of Dorset. Just to the west of Dorchester and down to the sea is the Abbotsbury Garden. As you come down off the A35 from Winterbourne Abbas, past the Hardy Monument towards the sea, you suddenly have this thrill of seeing the ocean. Dorset has one of the most picturesque coasts in all of England. The village of Abbotsbury has been famous for its swannery for centuries but in more recent times is also famous for its subtropical garden. The gardens are just past the village, heading west and down Bullers Way going down to the sea. It's all well signposted and easy to find. The garden has a long history, first created back in the 1760s by the first Countess of Ilchester, and the garden is still in the same family today.

Blessed with one of the best climates in England and sheltered from the nearby sea, the gardeners are able to grow a host of exotic greenery from Australia, New Zealand and South Africa. Adding to the exotic flavour is a collection of palm trees. The gardens are protected overhead by huge old oaks and the shape of the valley helps shelter things even more, so any coastal gales are excluded. The climate is virtually frost-free and very mild by English standards. The warm wet westerlies bring rain throughout the year, averaging 120 in (3 m) a year.

The garden has a few older big-leaf rhododendrons but in recent times they have planted a collection of big-leafs as a memorial to the late John Bond who was in charge of the Savill and Windsor gardens for many years. John was incredibly knowledgeable and always willing to share his time and knowledge with younger enthusiasts. This collection of large-leaf rhododendrons was planted in conjunction with the RHS Rhododendron Group and is a fitting tribute to a great plantsman.

Abbotsbury Subtropical Gardens, England.

Many of these plants are grown from seed from collections made by local people such as Tom Hudson, Edward Needham, Alan Clark and Keith Rushforth. For instance there's a *R. suoilenhense* AC431 collected by Alan Clark in Vietnam, and a *R. kesangiae* KR 1737 collected by Keith Rushforth in Bhutan. So this is a collection to watch for the future because nearly all of the plants are gathered by modern enthusiasts reconnoitring the Himalayas rather than simply repropagating old Forrest and Ernest Wilson material.

CAERHAYS CASTLE

Gorran, St Austell, Cornwall, PL26 6LY

www.caerhays.co.uk

The magnificent Caerhays Castle was built for the Trevanion family by the famous architect John Nash in 1810. The huge expense eventually bankrupted them and they fled to Europe to escape their creditors.

Then in 1855 Michael Williams acquired the Castle and planted many trees, but the garden collection as we know it today began in earnest around 1900. The owner at the time, John Charles Williams, 1861–1939, usually known as J.C., was Michael's grandson. He began growing rhododendron hybrids and was persuaded by the Veitch Nurseries in nearby Devon to grow some of the new rhododendrons grown from seed collected in China by E.H. Wilson.

J.C. subsequently became besotted with rhododendrons and employed George Forrest to collect for him in China. From 1911 to his death in 1932, Forrest was funded in part or in full by

Williams and the Caerhays Garden. It is unlikely Forrest would have been able to continue collecting without J.C. Williams' support. Naturally this arrangement meant the Caerhays Garden had access to the newest and best rhododendrons coming out of China during this period.

It was gardening on a grand scale as he had over fifty gardeners at one point. Nowadays the garden is managed by a more modest team of four or five for an area of around 120 acres (50 hectares). It is not a manicured garden but rather a natural woodland garden, as J.C. tried to create a natural setting for his wild Yunnan rhododendrons.

The garden also benefited from other Forrest collections such as maples, primulas and magnolias: it has the national collection for magnolias. All this is helped by a unique microclimate. The region is warm, wet and windy but the trees and terrain protect the garden from the worst of the gales. The warm Gulf Stream brings frequent rain and good gardening weather throughout the year.

TRENGWAINTON GARDENS

Nr. Penzance, Cornwall TR20 8RZ

ww.nationaltrust.org.uk/trengwainton-garden

This property has a long history dating back to the sixteenth century. In gardening terms, we're mostly interested in the man who began planting the trees. Rose Price, slave owner and sugar magnate from Jamaica, bought the property in 1814. He built the walled gardens and organised much of the tree planting. The twin purpose was to protect the gardens from the strong winds and to provide sunny aspects plus additional heat from the walls to grow tender plants. When slavery was abolished in 1833, it left his family nearly destitute. Much later, in 1867, a banker called Bolitho bought the property and it was one of his descendants, Sir Edward Bolitho, who created the garden we see today, beginning in 1925 when he inherited the estate.

Trengwainton is a Cornish word for a farm or settlement which has been well sited close to an underground water supply or spring. In some ways the garden could be described as being in constant spring with the warm Gulf Stream bringing warm temperatures and regular rainfall. Those early trees planted by Rose Price and others give shelter from the Atlantic winds. The garden is nearly 100 acres (40 hectares) of sheltered woodland and walled enclosures. It's famous for the rhododendrons and also camellias and magnolias and is also blessed with spectacular views of St Michael's Mount.

In 1926, Bolitho helped fund the Frank Kingdon Ward 1927–1928 seed-collecting trip to north-east Assam and the Mishmi Hills in upper Burma. Kingdon Ward collected a good swag of rhododendron which suited the Trengwainton climate and *R. macabeanum*, *R. elliottii*, and *R. taggianum* all flowered for the first time in Britain in this garden.

Today the garden has a semi-tropical feel with tree ferns and palms, and is host to many rare and exotic plants from the southern hemisphere. The property is now owned by the National Trust and open to the public from mid-February to the end of October.

AUSTRALIA AND NEW ZEALAND

NATIONAL RHODODENDRON GARDENS

The Georgian Rd, Olinda, Australia

parkweb.vic.gov.au/explore/parks/national-rhododendron-garden

In 1960 some members of the Ferny Creek Horticultural Society decided to form the Australian Rhododendron Society. They asked the Forests Commission for some land to begin a rhododendron garden and were granted a 50-acre (20-hectare) site, later doubled to 100 acres (40 hectare) in 1975. The piece of land they chose was in the Olinda State Forest on the side of Mt Dandenong on the outskirts of Melbourne.

Twenty years later, in 1995, the National Rhododendron Gardens became part of the Melbourne Parks department now known as Parks Victoria. The gardens are home to literally thousands of rhododendrons, azaleas, camellias and a host of cherries and magnolias. They also have a host of Vireya rhododendrons.

It's the ideal climate with a misty cool-mountain atmosphere ideally suited to rhododendrons. The backdrop of giant mountain ash, *Eucalyptus regnans*, is impressive as this species is the tallest flowering plant in the world and comparable in majesty to the Californian redwoods. The garden enjoys memorable views over the Yarra Valley below and are designed as a series of rooms or spaces, with the rhododendrons in each blended into their surroundings. Besides many hybrids, they also have a stunning collection of big-leaf tree rhododendrons under high-canopy eucalyptus.

The soil is perfect — free-draining deep volcanic clay loam, and acid in nature. Average annual rainfall is around 40 in (1000 mm) but the soil is moisture-retentive, plus the cool atmosphere reduces evaporation. Wind is rarely a problem.

High summer temperatures coupled with lowering rainfall have caused concern in recent years, and more irrigation is needed. Fire risk has also been extreme at times.

EMU VALLEY RHODODENDRON GARDEN

Cascade Rd, Romaine, Burnie, Tasmania, Australia

www.emuvalleyrhodo.com.au

North-west Tasmania, with its soft climate and reliable rainfall, is perfect for gardening. The climate is cool enough to enjoy four distinct seasons but mild enough to grow Himalayan plants to perfection. The Emu Valley Rhododendron Garden is a natural amphitheatre blessed with rich volcanic soil. It all slopes down with various streams and rills to create lakes and waterfalls in a moist atmosphere ideally suited to rhododendron culture.

The 30-acre (12-hectare) garden was the brainchild of three rhododendron men back in 1981. The landowner, Hilary O'Rourke, was a breeder, Bob Malone a nurseryman and Noel Sullivan, an enthusiast. It is now owned and managed by the Emu Valley Rhododendron Society, a voluntary non-profit organisation. The site was not very appealing in those early days as it was mostly cut-over scrub, but these three enthusiasts knew the climate and soil were perfect.

Emu Valley Rhododendron Garden, Tasmania, Australia.

Nowadays the garden is set out to display rhododendrons from different regions and countries of the world. Some describe the garden as a plant museum. Part of their aim is to preserve rhododendrons which may be endangered in the wild. With over 20,000 rhododendrons they have gone quite some way towards this aim. Graham Smith, Director of Pukeiti, sent seed of his large-leaf hybrids to them and many of the plants are now flowering superbly in the early spring.

The garden is open daily from the beginning of August, when the big-leafs flower, to the end of April. They also have a collection of Vireya rhododendrons under a woodland canopy of *Acacia melanoxylon*.

Below: Pukeiti Rhododendron Trust, New Plymouth, New Zealand.

PUKEITI RHODODENDRON TRUST

2290 Carrington Rd, RD4, New Plymouth, New Zealand

www.trc.govt.nz/pukeiti-rhododendron-trust

The dream of one man and the sweat of many others has created Pukeiti over the last sixty years. In 1950, Douglas Cook, the founder of the Eastwoodhill Arboretum near Gisborne, decided he wanted to create a rhododendron garden and chose the province of Taranaki on the wet west coast of the North Island as the perfect site. The Gisborne region was too hot and dry for rhododendrons. He was shown the Pukeiti site, promptly bought it and then set about creating a Trust with like-minded foundation members, and subsequently many other volunteers.

Over the next sixty years the foundation members and many new recruits have cut swathes in the native bush to plant and establish a huge collection of rhododendrons, possibly the most diverse collection in the world: everything from tender Vireya rhododendrons from Borneo and New Guinea right through to huge tree big-leaf monsters.

The gardens were initially laid out by master craftsman Jack Goodwin who anticipated the phenomenal growth of rhododendrons in this wet climate and spaced everything miles apart. Then, in 1969, a bright (eyed) young Kew graduate, Graham Smith, became the curator. Graham, the co-author of this book, went on to become one of the foremost authorities on rhododendrons in the world.

Nowadays, Pukeiti boasts the best collection of big-leaf rhododendrons in the world. The climate is wet, very wet, often exceeding 144 in (4 m) a year, but otherwise it's a very mild climate allowing such a magnificent collection to thrive.

In 2010, the garden was taken over by the Taranaki Regional Council who work in conjunction with the pre-existing Trust to manage the gardens.

GWAVAS GARDEN

5740 Highway 50, Tikokino, Hawke's Bay, New Zealand

www.gwavasgarden.co.nz

The property was bought by Major George Gwavas Carlyon of Tregrehan in Par, Cornwall when he first came to New Zealand. The 22-acre (9-hectare) garden was originally laid out in the 1880s by A.S.G. Carlyon. The current owner, Michael Hudson, is his grandson. Michael and his wife Carola have created a woody plant Mecca beneath this canopy of mature trees. This has been a labour of love over the last five decades.

Upper drive, Gwavas Garden, Hawke's Bay, New Zealand.

Michael has an absolute passion for plants and in the days before import restrictions was regularly buying plants from Hilliers and other nurseries in England. The Gwavas Garden can be likened to *Hilliers Manual* in the flesh as virtually every plant in the *Manual* can be found here.

The garden is constantly updated with new and exciting material. In the '80s and '90s New Zealand had a mini-Renaissance with lots of people exploring the world and introducing new plants. Michael Hudson was at the forefront of this and any new plants were soon established at Gwavas. In recent times, government restrictions have since stopped all plant imports thus making the Gwavas collection even more important.

Michael's son, Tom Hudson of the Tregrehan estate in Cornwall, is following in his father's footsteps. Prior to 1997 when these import restrictions were instituted, Tom, who is a modern-day collector, brought back a wealth of new plants from China, Vietnam and Bhutan, many of which are now thriving in the Gwavas Garden.

Many of the rhododendrons in the collection are numbered clones collected by George Forrest, Kingdon Ward, the Coxes and others. For such a dry climate, Michael has worked miracles to grow many of the big-leaf rhododendrons. The annual rainfall is low, around 40 in (1000 mm).

The property is about 1000 feet above sea level and this makes it cooler at night during the summer months. This is critical for rhododendron health in this hot, dry region. Also there are huge shelter trees around the property giving shade and shelter to the big-leafs.

CHAPTER 8

Growing rhododendrons successfully

When blessed with an acid, free-draining soil and regular rainfall throughout the year, rhododendrons are fairly easy to grow. But if we add in factors like shelter from strong winds or not too much hot sun, then gradually the picture becomes more complicated. In most cases gardeners have to modify some aspect of their soil or climate to improve their chances of growing healthy happy rhododendrons.

But as any true gardener knows, we all love a challenge. Once you have grown a selection of rhododendrons and find out more about them it's naturally tempting to want to grow the kings of the genus. Big-leaf rhododendrons are even more pernickety because they need more shelter from wind and hot sun; plus, they seem to pine for their Himalayan homeland where every second day is a wet day. And to top it off, many of them flower so early in the season which puts the flowers at more risk from frosts.

SOIL AND DRAINAGE

Good drainage is essential and without it, it is nigh on impossible to grow rhododendrons. In the wild many of them grow on rocky slopes and form a mat of roots across the surface. In some places, they seem to be growing on peat bogs but invariably the water is moving rather than stagnant. It's a peculiar thing but many plants can cope with wet soil if the water is moving as there is still air in the root zone, whereas in stagnant water, there is no air available to the roots. Gardeners are always aware their plants need water but rarely think about the roots needing air as well. Without air in the root zone the plants will suffocate and die.

R. protistum 'Pukeiti'.

The other problem associated with wet feet is the threat of the root disease *Phytophthora*. This pernicious fungus is spread by water within the root zone but always seems to be more prevalent after heavy rain or in poorly drained regions. If the drainage in your chosen site is not perfect, there are several things you can do to help overcome the problem.

In the wild, many rhododendrons grow as epiphytes and seemingly all of them appreciate and need good drainage. I knew an experienced rhododendron grower who, on seeing a seedy plant, especially one that was beginning to wilt from phytophthora disease, would promptly dig up the plant and set it on the ground next to the hole. Decades later, many of these plants are still thriving and you can still recognise the block of soil that contained the roots he dug up. Only problem was he didn't fill in the holes, and it's a minor miracle no one broke their ankle. Aside from this unusual method, however, there are basically two or three things you can do to improve drainage: one is by installing drains or adding extra, open material to the soil mix. The alternative is to grow the rhododendrons in a raised mound or constructed bed.

Let's look at soil improvement first. Installing permanent drains is expensive and not always successful. In the process you are disturbing the soil layers and may cause more problems than you solve. If the drainage in your site is so bad you need permanent drains it may be better to look elsewhere on your property for a site to grow rhododendrons. As for adding material, any large particles such as sand, perlite, pumice or chunky peat will improve the drainage when mixed with existing soil.

If you have a clay soil then adding gypsum (calcium sulphate) will improve the drainage. Gypsum is a form of calcium which fortunately does not increase the pH or lime content of the soil very much, and it does not damage rhododendrons. What it does do is to make the clay particles stick together to form bigger pieces of soil, thus allowing more water and air to penetrate.

Another way of improving the drainage, and possibly the best long-term solution, is to add plenty of organic matter. This will encourage worms and a host of soil fauna, and their endeavours will gradually turn poorly structured soils into a friable, free-draining medium. In the wild, rhododendrons enjoy growing in cool mossy montane forest. These regions have low fertility and this gives the rhododendrons a competitive advantage because they can outgrow other plants. In our gardens we want large healthy plants capable of flowering every year and so we need to increase the availability of the organic matter to feed and encourage the plant.

Use well-rotted compost or animal manure. Horse or cow manure, especially mixed with a rough material like straw, is perfect as long as it is not too fresh. Fresh manure can kill the roots of choice plants. Chicken manure is very strong when fresh and will almost certainly damage your plants. Most people think you have to dig in any compost or manure but the reality is, nature does it best. Just lay the material on the surface and the worms and soil fauna will do the job for you. Every time you dig you change the patterns for the soil fauna. Each creature has a niche at a certain level and by digging you literally turn their world upside down and kill most of them. Seaweed is another magic ingredient if you have ready access to it. While it seems to rot away in a matter of days, the subsequent improvement in soil texture is incredible. By these methods of improving the soil drainage, any excess water flows away much faster and the roots will have more air available to keep them healthy.

If your soil is poor or rocky, or perhaps a heavy clay, you may need to create a special environment for the roots of your treasured rhododendron. This is more successful if it's done on sloping ground where any excess water can flow away. You can do this with natural pine logs which will rot after a while, adding to the soil structure. Make a three or four-sided frame from rough-sawn timber or natural logs. It doesn't matter what you use to make the frame, although whole timber logs with bark still attached looks more natural.

The frame needs to be at least a metre square and probably a lot more for tree rhododendrons. Pin the frame to the ground using stakes and nails. Fill the box with good free-draining soil and perhaps add potting mix to improve it. Now the one drawback having given your plant the perfect drainage is that it may now be too dry, as this light, open mix on top of the ground will soon lose moisture. You are trying to grow the plant like an epiphyte as it might do in the wild. However, without enough rain, you may need to install a temporary irrigation system until the plants are established.

As we have seen, rhododendrons like good drainage. Even if your climate doesn't bring them all the rainfall they desire, they still need good drainage for the times when it is wet around the roots. If your soil drainage is adequate or good, then we can look at ways of improving the plants' environment.

ACIDITY AND FERTILISER

We know rhododendrons prefer acid soil even though many of them grow on limestone in the wild. In areas such as Lijiang in China or parts of Tibet the natural soil they grow on is limestone. George Forrest was particularly keen to share this information with gardeners back home in Britain. However, the limestone in these regions is not everyday limestone but rather the harder, more resilient dolomite. Dolomite has a high percentage of magnesium and rhododendrons in our garden enjoy a dollop of dolomite or magnesium. Dolomite is slow to break down in comparison with ordinary lime or chalk.

While rhododendrons have adapted to live in low-fertility sites, they do respond to artificial fertilisers and will provide you with healthier foliage and better crops of flowers. However, you can overdo it and make the plant too lush for the overall climate, making the plant susceptible to harsh winter weather. The answer is to feed sparingly but on an annual basis.

It's tempting to think the modern slow-release fertilisers are good for all plants, but they are usually temperature related. The warmer the temperatures, the greater and faster the release of nutrients. What this does is give the plant the maximum nutrient load in late summer, thus encouraging late soft growth which is more liable to be damaged by frost. Better by far is to make your own recipe using cheaper ingredients and applying in spring when the plant most needs the nutrients for a new set of leaves and formation of next year's flower buds.

An NPK ratio of 12:6:6 mix is ideal. This is 12% nitrogen, 6% phosphate and 6% potassium. Nitrogen is best applied in ammonium forms which are fast-acting, rather than nitrate, which is slower to release. There is a danger of ammonium forms burning the roots, so make sure you spread the mix evenly across the surface.

Superphosphate makes the soil more alkaline, which is not good for rhododendrons, so go for the more simple phosphates. Phosphate encourages flower-bud production. Potash in the form of potassium sulphate helps the plant stay healthy as it hardens the growth, making them more resistant to inclement weather, pests and diseases.

If your soil is slightly limey or even neutral, you may want to try to acidify it. Sulphur at 4 oz per square yard (125 g per square metre) will reduce the pH. Putting iron on the soil will also reduce the pH. Chelated iron or iron sulphate at 1 oz per square yard (20 g per square metre) will help.

As mentioned before, gypsum is good for improving the texture of soils and also encouraging the releases of certain nutrients. Dolomite lime has a similar action and has the added benefit of giving magnesium, which makes the plant greener and healthier. All these nutrients mentioned in this paragraph help alleviate chlorosis, when leaves look pale or yellow. They all encourage the greening of leaves by making magnesium more available to the plant.

Like us, plants like a varied diet and we all need trace elements, including our rhododendrons. It's possible to buy trace elements as a ready-made mix, sometimes called frits.

Of course, it goes without saying that natural or created compost is one of the best food sources for plants. If you have enough time and energy to create or gather natural compost then use this to feed your plants.

MULCHING

The next best thing you can do for your rhododendrons is to provide a thick layer of mulch around the base of the plant. Rhododendrons simply love having mulch around them. This keeps the soil and the roots cool. It has the remarkable effect of making the soil cooler in summer and warmer in winter, both of which is advantageous for our prized plants.

Mulch also reduces evaporation, thus keeping the soil moist for longer. Rhododendrons are especially appreciative because they are surface-rooting. Many plants send their roots deep into the soil to find water and nutrients, while rhododendrons have nearly all of their roots in the top foot (30 cm) of the soil profile. This is apparent when you dig up a large rhododendron. If you have the right lifting equipment or sufficient manpower, you can more or less peel them out of the ground.

The perfect mulch is crushed pine bark from a mill, deposited between 2–4 in (5–10 cm) deep. The mulch should go out to the edge of the drip line, or in the case of a young plant, well beyond the drip line to encourage new roots to spread further. Pine bark is slow to rot down and so it lasts a long time. It is also very open, allowing free exchange of air, and permits water and rain to percolate through quite easily.

R. protistum seedling hybrids at Pukeiti.

Depending on your locality, there may be products such as pea straw, seaweed, cocoa bean husk, or spent peach stones which you can employ as mulch. Some people recommend sawdust, but there are two or three major drawbacks. One, the sawdust tends to pack down really hard and it then becomes impervious to water and operates like a thatch roof. And when it's packed down hard, it is more difficult for air to circulate. Thirdly, because of the small particles of wood, the sawdust breaks down more quickly than bark, and in the process it robs the soil of nitrogen. Any rotting material such as straw, sawdust and bark will take nitrogen from the soil to speed the decomposition, but in the case of sawdust this happens much faster. Wheat and barley straws create a similar problem whereas pea straw has nitrogen within, so it's not so problematic.

Gardeners with established old trees can mulch every day as they walk by. Shade the soil by throwing old sticks and branches around the base of your plant, and in time tumbling leaves will gather around these sticks, creating a wholesome mulch or compost.

CLIMATE — SHADE, SHELTER AND WIND

Shade is brilliant because it modifies the temperature at two key seasons for our rhododendrons. It saves them from the cruel hot sun of summer, but just as crucial is the effect of minimising frost damage in the spring when the flowers and new leaves are emerging. Frost is always more severe and more deadly in open paddocks than it is under a canopy of tall trees. Even if the plants do get frost on them, the slow melting process in a shady situation is much safer than a quick hot sun melt which can devastate rhododendrons and magnolias.

Another factor often neglected is that rhododendrons, especially big-leafs, don't like hot sun on their root zone. If there is no protection from overhead trees, or shade from the plant's own canopy or from a mulch, the soil will be hotter and drier. Because rhododendrons have all their roots near the surface, the roots get cooked, and dry out without the benefit of shade.

Depending on your terrain you may be able to use slopes to advantage to provide their own shade. If you plant your rhododendrons on a slope facing your nearest pole, i.e. away from the sun, then the land is naturally shaded. Northern hemisphere gardeners should plant on north-facing slopes to shield the roots and soil from hot sun. Slopes are beneficial in others way, too. Because frost moves like water, or rather like liquid nitrogen at a rock concert, it flows to the lowest point. So having all your rhododendrons at the bottom of a dell is not a good idea; rather, you should choose somewhere halfway up the slope because the frost flows through them and settles somewhere down below.

Orchardists are much more aware of how to handle frost and they will remove the lower branches on the shelter belts or hedges at the bottom of the orchard. This allows the frost to keep moving on down the slope in to the neighbour's property. Frost also fills up a hollow, so even being near the bottom is not safe because as the dell or bowl fills with frost, plants higher up the slope are enveloped in damaging frosty air. Make the effort and walk about your property on frosty nights to observe where frost flows and settles. Rapid freezing is far worse than slow freezing. Likewise rapid melting is more dangerous to the plant than gradual melting of frost and ice. Frost can cause disfigurement such as distorted tips of the leaves, or if too severe, can wreck the leaves completely. Expanding buds, flowers and new leaves are, of course, the most sensitive to damage. Frozen ground is a serious problem, too, because your plants cannot access any water when the ground freezes.

Some climates, like in Korea, have a very gradual increase of cold in autumn and a very sedate slow increase of temperatures in the spring. This gradual slope down then up again is perfect for plants because they 'know' every day will be a little cooler as winter approaches and can adjust. Similarly in spring the plant knows tomorrow will be a little warmer than today.

Britain by comparison has a haywire climate. It can be warm in February and March, tempting the plants into growth only to be sideswiped by a late frost. Again, your shade trees can help the situation by keeping the garden cool in February to March, negating these false springs. Likewise Britain can be cold in summer and it's very confusing for plants. *Hilliers Manual of Trees and Shrubs* frequently mentions how hard it is to grow Korean and Manchurian plants because of the haphazard weather patterns in the UK, and the false springs.

Frosts in autumn or spring are usually far more dramatic and damaging than midwinter frosts. In midwinter the plant has virtually shut down and knows it's going to be cold and is prepared for it. In the wild some rhododendrons regularly roll their leaves like cigars as a defence against cold and dehydration and can remain in that state for months until the spring thaw gradually eases the conditions and a sudden late freeze is unlikely. This condition is not quite the same as drought or heat stress in the garden situation where water and shade deficiencies are a result of the artificial environment.

Another oft-forgotten factor of having shade and or shelter trees is that they protect plants from severe winds, especially from drying winds. Strong or constant winds can and will dehydrate your treasured plants and cause them to sulk, or even die. Rhododendrons hate regular or constant winds, and while they can put up with an occasional storm, it's the persistent winds that do the most damage. Wind every day is far more damaging than one severe gale. Wind can be good, though, and can be a saviour when it's frosty. Wind or even a strong breeze can move frost along or deny it a place to settle.

Heat causes its own problems, such as dry soil, causing buds to fail and leaves to wilt. Less severe but still disfiguring is that the leaves may go yellow and anaemic. The hotter and drier the climate, the greater the need for overhead shade. Big-leaf rhododendrons need shade in most regions but it's definitely essential in areas with high sunshine hours and dry climates. Obviously this is more of a problem during the hottest months, July and August in the northern hemisphere and January and February in the southern hemisphere. Try to site your plants so they get the benefit of shade during this critical period, as it's the most crucial time.

There is also the factor of 'used to it'. If the plants in your garden are used to periods of hot dry conditions they will cope better than a friend's garden in a mild moist climate which endures a sudden and out-of-character heat wave. Naturally inland areas are much hotter, especially in Europe and America where continental hot summers and freezing cold winters are the norm. Even maritime climates like Britain and New Zealand have much hotter temperatures inland. Gardens near the coast are doubly blessed with warm mild winters and cool soft summers.

Lakes and ponds have a moderating effect on microclimates, making the nearby environment cooler in summer and warmer in winter. Altitude can help, too, though we can't change what we have. Just being 1000 feet above sea level means cooler nights, which encourages rhododendrons.

If we study where they live naturally then we get a better idea of what they need in cultivation. In general rhododendrons like a moist mild climate, with high rainfall. This is even more pronounced for the big-leaf giant rhododendrons because any hint of drought will put them under stress. In the moist rainforest where many of these big-leaf species grow naturally, there is a tendency for plants to grow epiphytically on other plants. While this may be perfect for the plants involved, this kind of climate is not pleasant for us. Most of us live in a better drier climate, and so we have to try to modify our drier climate for these choice plants.

If you want to grow big-leaf or tree rhododendrons, you have to look at your climate. The hotter and drier your region, the more difficult it will be grow them to perfection. This applies to virtually all rhododendrons but especially to the big-leaf monsters. Most of the desirable tree-like rhododendrons come from high altitudes, growing on the slopes of misty mountains. This means they are accustomed to seeing rain for half the days of a calendar year. Naturally they will cope with less, but they still need regular rainfall and a humid climate to thrive. High rainfall equals lower sunshine hours and this helps because of the corresponding cooler temperatures, suiting the plants.

Jiaozishan in north-east Yunnan showing mixed rhododendrons, including *R. rex* ssp. *rex* and *Abies georgei*.

In their native habitat, these misty and rainy days not only bring moisture but also shade from the hot sun. Thus the number of sunshine hours per year is low and the plants are naturally protected from scorching or drying. In a garden situation where there are numerous misty days such as at Pukeiti in New Zealand, many of the giant rhododendrons are growing out in full sun. However, the sheer number of misty days means their sunshine hours are probably half of what they are just a few kilometres away at sea level. Therefore if you have a sunny climate, overhead shade becomes even more important.

Try to give the plants ample shade from the hot sun by choosing a location under big trees. The perfect setting is under tall deciduous trees such as oaks and ash. Pines make good shade trees, too. If your climate allows, then magnolia trees are a fantastic shade tree because they have big searching roots and virtually none on the surface to compete with rhododendrons. Ideally you want the trees to give dappled shade throughout the hottest parts of the day. So before you begin planting, look to see the trajectory of the sun and place the rhododendrons in the spot most shaded in the early afternoon when the sun is at its hottest. Obviously this varies depending on whether you are in the northern or southern hemisphere, and also your latitude, so you have to study your own situation in high summer. The advantage of deciduous trees, like oaks, is they lose their leaves in winter, allowing more light to filter through when the sun is low and the

GROWING RHODODENDRONS SUCCESSFULLY

temperatures are cooler. Hopefully your high trees are species with deep roots so they will not be competing with the roots of your shrubs. Another benefit of having deciduous trees is they drop their leaves, providing a generous layer of natural compost or mulch.

Regarding shelter from cold winds, choose a site in the lee of the shelter, thus protecting the plants from the worst of the wind. If you do not have sufficient shelter from the wind, then either try to establish a hedge or shelter break of wind-hardy plants. The other alternative is to create a filter using 'wind cloth' or a fence of some kind. Our favourite big-leafs are even more prone to wind damage because the leaves are so big and they literally catch the wind.

Which brings me to how best we can help rhododendrons get established in our gardens. What follows here is applicable to most rhododendrons but especially so to the big-leaf varieties. Species rhododendrons and especially big-leafs are happier in shade. This is especially true when the plant is young. Often you just need a 'nurse' shrub or tree to protect the young rhododendron. If you have some trees or shrubs which are not especially valuable, you can use these as the immediate shade and shelter for the young rhododendron. As the plant becomes more established, you can reduce or remove the 'nurse' plant.

IRRIGATION AND WATER PRESERVATION.

Most places where gardeners try to grow big-leaf rhododendrons are naturally wet climates, but there are always times when the heavens don't deliver. Kingdon Ward talked about how hillsides of wild rhododendrons suffered or even died in severe droughts. In his book *Rhododendrons for Everyone* he talks of acres of rhododendrons without a flower and several instances of big-leaf colonies deprived of flowers due to drought.

Experienced gardeners know rhododendrons can cope with severe drought because the leaves curl or roll in cigar fashion to conserve moisture. When this happens the plant is likely to abort any developing flower buds. When the moisture returns, the plants usually bounce back to seeming full health in a very short time. But undoubtedly the plant will have lost condition, lost a portion of the leaves and quite likely lose any developing flower buds. Even extremely cold weather can act like a drought because the plant can't access water from the root zone where the roots are inactive.

Before we think of irrigating, we should first investigate any ways of preserving moisture in the soil. The most obvious way is to apply a thick mulch of bark or wood chips. Before you set up an irrigation system, take a close look at your water supply. If it's bore water it's worth getting it tested to assess the nutrient status. It may be alkaline and if so will hinder rather than help your precious rhododendrons. In some regions, the tap water has come from limestone areas and is known as 'hard water' (acid water is known as 'soft'). Look inside your electric jug or kettle. If the inside of the jug has a thick white layer over the element, then you have hard, limey water.

Ironically, rhododendrons often flower in less than perfect conditions. It seems if they are stressed, they react by producing flowers whereas plants grown under perfect conditions often say thank you and produce luxuriant foliage at the expense of flowers.

CULTIVATION, DEADHEADING AND PRUNING

Once you've found your perfect site, planted your big-leafs and given them an ample mulch, well it's all done, isn't it? Not really. Over the first few years you need to keep a close eye on them. Firstly, make sure they don't dry out especially at the root zone and keep them as cool as possible. Apply regular top-ups of mulch and water, or in extreme cases install an irrigation system.

In these early years you need to keep them free of weeds for several reasons. One is the obvious aesthetic value as weeds are not a good look. But, more importantly, weeds compete for moisture and nutrients.

Pulling weeds by hand tends to bring up clods of earth or mulch, and also encourages new weeds to grow. A heavy mulch is the best way to deter weeds. If you are not opposed for philosophical or environmental reasons, then perhaps herbicides are the least invasive way of controlling the weeds. Ideally spray them before they get too big and definitely before they begin flowering and spreading their seeds.

As for pruning, in general rhododendrons do not need pruning and this applies to the big-leafs as well. Typically they have a good natural rounded shape. While the plant is young, there's an opportunity to shape it and avoid problems later. The most obvious is having two branches very close together. As they grow and enlarge, they compete for the same space and may rub together, causing a weak spot. Naturally any dead or diseased wood needs to be removed.

Old established rhododendrons can be drastically pruned to revitalise them. Most species and cultivars tolerate and even enjoy being cut back to bare wood with a chainsaw. The exception is any plant with a smooth stem. It seems the rough bark species and cultivars regenerate but for some reason the smooth bark ones such as the *R. maddenii* series and the big 'Loderi' cultivars will often die. Many of our big-leaf tree rhododendrons have rough bark and so they could be cut back like this but it's unlikely you will ever need to be this cruel.

On a more mundane level, there is a type of pruning which encourages good health and a better flower display. Deadheading is a form of pruning and essential to encourage your plants to flower every year. Rhododendrons usually produce so much seed the poor plant is diminished and weakened. Big-leaf rhododendrons are no different in this aspect. If you look at an older established bush which has flowered, it tends to send up two or three weak shoots from below the seed cases. If you remove the spent flower within a week or two of flowering, then the plant will put out much stronger, longer growth which in turn is far more likely to flower next season. One strange side effect of removing the spent flowers is the new leaves will be bigger. Obviously the effort of producing seeds takes energy from the plant and so the leaves are smaller.

In effect, rhododendrons are biennial bearers like many apples, plums and pears. Many of the giant rhododendrons tend to bear flowers every other year, sometimes taking a two-year rest between flowerings. The effort of producing fruit so depletes the plant it does not flower well the next season. This is largely due to overproduction of seeds and by deadheading soon after the flowers have faded you give the plant a chance to rebuild its reserves and also put energy into next year's flowers. Orchardists overcome this problem by winter-pruning to reduce the potential fruit numbers, and then in early summer by fruit-thinning.

With our rhododendrons we don't want to reduce the flowering in any one season, but we do want the plant to flower well every season. Deadheading after flowering helps them flower every year. It's an easy task, if a slightly messy one. Using one or two forefingers to hold the spent truss you flick the seed head off with your thumb. The seed cases are usually sticky and the greasy mess sticks to your fingers. No need to pick up the spent case, let them rot on the ground.

Our big-leaf rhodos are easy to deadhead when young and the bush is small but it becomes a real problem when the bush gets above head high. Then you are left with three choices. One is do nothing and have a good set of flowers every second year. You could get a ladder or perhaps the best technique is use the blade on a long-handled hand saw to just put pressure on the seed case until it flicks off. In the long term these plants become trees and deadheading is impossible except on the lower branches and you have to accept that flowering may be reduced some years. When you might have waited for twenty years to see the first flower, any flowering is special.

Another factor regarding flowering that is often overlooked is the delaying effect on the new growth. A bush with no flowers will come into leaf several weeks before a bush that was laden with flowers. This can be critical in terms of reducing frost damage because the danger of frosts may be over if the growth comes later.

PESTS AND DISEASES

Pests and diseases can be a problem. For some reason, pests and diseases appear to attack unhappy plants rather than healthy ones, so the logic is, if you maintain the health of your plants, they are less likely to be attacked. It does appear to be an odd contradiction, as why would you, or in this case a pest, prefer to eat a deficient specimen over a healthy one.

While there are several things which attack rhododendrons, not many seem to strike the big-leaf species. The two biggest problems are forms of phytophthora. *P. cinnamomi* causes root rot and this is mostly due to poor drainage or very heavy rain. Good drainage is the key to preventing this disease. If your plant shows symptoms of phytophthora such as drooping or unhappy leaves, then you could sprinkle a proprietary phosphorus acid powder on the root zone or spray the plant leaves with it.

In southern England a new species, *P. ramorum*, has established itself recently. Known as Sudden Oak Death, it kills rhododendrons but surprisingly not English oaks. This disease was first noticed in California and Oregon in the early '90s and is gradually spreading to the east coast of the USA and to Europe. This form attacks the leaves of the plant, so it can be contained, unlike the soil-borne disease.

Perhaps a better and longer-lasting solution is to inject your trees with Agrimm Trichodowels. These are like the wall plugs to hold a picture on your wall and they contain the *Trichoderma* or 'good-guy' fungi which outmuscle the phytophthora fungi. They don't actually kill the bad fungus; they simply fill up the spaces and take the place of them.

Thankfully few pests ever bother rhododendrons and especially our big-leafs. Thrips can attack the surface of the leaves in warm climates and usually when they are young plants but it's uncommon. In most cases the undersides of the leaves are protected by the thick layers of indumentum. The thrips don't like indumentum as it's a physical barrier to their mode of operation.

Stem borers can do a lot of damage for a single caterpillar. The adult moth lays an egg on the branch and the tiny caterpillar bores into the trunk. At night they emerge from the middle of the trunk to start eating the bark around the branch, making a circle, and eventually they ring-bark the stem. These clever beasts cover their track with a netting of cobweb and debris to make it look as if the trunk is intact. You need to catch them in the early stage before they complete the circle and kill the branch. Keen observation is the only way to find them. For some reason some large-leafs, in particular *R. sinogrande*, are susceptible to stem borer if they are present and regular inspection is necessary.

There are several cures: one is to carry a can of car engine starter, stick the nozzle into the main hole into the trunk and give it a squirt. The toxic gasoline-like liquid sends them out pretty quick. Another simple method is to sharpen a dead stick and jam it tightly into the hole. This traps them inside where they die. It must be a dead stick as they can chew their way through a live stick.

Probably the most common pests are weevils. These horrible creatures can do serious damage. Some species have larvae attacking the roots and so the damage is occurring unseen below ground level. The adults tend to climb the stems to partake of the leaves, chewing the leaf edges and causing unsightly notches along the leaf blade. The adults can be deterred by wrapping tape around the trunks, so their tiny feet cannot grip and climb. Another similar technique involves dabbing a proprietary sticky barrier to the trunks, trapping the little monsters as they climb to do their mischief, but these barrier materials are difficult to apply and remove.

These barriers must be applied to the trunk so there are no unprotected avenues of travel up the stalk. The weevils either will choose not to travel up the trunk or will become stuck in the barrier and thus cannot move into the canopy to feed. There are some indications that prolonged use of these materials can be somewhat damaging to the bark, so a strip of polyethylene, waterproof tape or thin plastic can be fitted tightly to the trunk and the sticky material applied to it. Plastic tape, etc., must be removed before trunk growth is restricted. The barrier materials can also be difficult to remove from tools or hands and so it is best to use gloves to apply. One rather pleasing technique is to make cylinders of corrugated cardboard and place these under the bushes. The weevils are likely to use these as daytime hidey places, as will slugs and snails. Every now and then dispose of the cylinders as you see fit.

Another avenue available in some countries is the use of nematode worms as a biological control. Some species of these tiny opaque worms attack the larvae of weevils. In a few places you can buy a paste containing a colony of these nematodes and introduce them to your soil. They have the advantage of being host-specific and they are not detrimental to the environment in any way.

The chemical arsenal you need to kill weevils is quite potent. As well as being unpleasant for you, they are likely to cause damage to beneficial insects and bees. Never spray your plants when they are in flower and attracting bees and other good insects.

CHAPTER 9

Propagating rhododendrons

Propagation of rhododendrons is seen as the domain of professionals, but there are several reasons why the general gardener might want to propagate their own. For a start, it's enjoyable and very satisfying to create new plants which you can then give away to like-minded friends. This is very important, especially if you have a rare or special rhododendron. We should all endeavour to propagate any valuable clones of plants we have in our gardens, particularly in the case of big-leaf rhododendrons, as it's often hard to find any suitable plants to purchase. If we can increase the number by cuttings, grafting or layering, we can enlarge our own collection for little or no cost, and hopefully have some to give away to friends.

The other possibility is to grow rhododendrons from seed. This may be a controlled crossing to create a new hybrid, or simply open pollinated seeds, which can give mixed results. Perhaps most importantly there is the opportunity to grow seed collected from the wild, and this may result in new forms or new clones or, if we are really lucky, it may be a new species.

Be aware that plants grown by asexual methods such as cuttings, layers and grafts will flower much sooner than seedling plants. This is because the material taken for asexual propagation is mature wood genetically programmed to flower, whereas seedlings are only interested in growing, not flowering.

Andrew Brooker preparing scions for grafting at Pukeiti.

HOW TO PROPAGATE THEM

SEEDS

The very first rhododendrons in cultivation had to be grown from seed. It was the only method in the initial collection era and it took the skills of the garden staff of private estates, botanical gardens and a few key nurseries to bring these unknowns into cultivation. In the case of the big-leaf rhododendrons, it was quite unknown just how long these regal plants would take to grow and eventually flower. Waiting for twenty-five to forty-five years for plants to flower was only going to be tolerated by those with huge planting areas, time, skill and patience. Probably tens of thousands of seedlings went by the wayside before many actually started to flower.

Nowadays, seeds can come from a variety of sources. If you have created your own hybrids by cross-pollination, then you need to keep very accurate records and have good labelling throughout the process. It can take several years from the first stage of pollinating through to having a plant big enough to put in the garden. It is unlikely that you will remember the parentage of your cross for this length of time, so be sure to label at every stage.

You may be lucky enough to have some wild seed, which you may have collected yourself on an expedition to rhododendron country. Or perhaps you have been given seed by someone who has travelled to distant lands. Some societies also put out a seed list for members to choose from and purchase.

The other possibility is that someone has given you seed from their plant. As this is from a cultivated plant, there is always the risk that the seed is of hybrid origin. You need to be sure and label them accordingly.

Rhododendron seed is usually small, about the size of a pinhead, very thin and light and easily blown away. Each capsule contains hundreds of seeds packed tightly together. Left in a warm dry place, these capsules usually open by themselves. Alternatively, you can either break the capsule in half with your fingers, or prise it open carefully with a knife. Be sure to tap out both ends to get all the seeds out.

Spring is a good time to sow the seeds, but any time from spring through till autumn is acceptable. Fill some small, squat pots with open free-draining potting mix. A combination of two or more of the following should suffice: peat, pumice, perlite, finely crushed pine bark or sand. Personally I prefer to use crushed pine bark which has been composted to remove the tannins. Soil mixes are risky because of the threat of disease and also because it may contain weed seeds. The key points are that it should be open and free-draining, but dense enough to hold moisture. You will need to add a layer of fertiliser about halfway down so the roots can access nutrients. Ideally, choose some long-term twelve to twenty-four-month slow-release fertiliser.

Tamp down the mix and make sure the surface is level. Then write a label describing the parentage, the source or location of the parent plant, and the day's date. Take the pot and the seed to the place where it will be for the next few months. If you sow the seed in one place and carry the pot to another, you may well have the seed blow off the top. It's better to water very gently and then sow the seed finely on top of the potting mix in situ where the pot will stay for the next few weeks, so decide where they are to go before you get started.

Sow the seed thinly as overcrowded seedlings are very prone to damping-off disease. Do not cover the seeds with potting mix or anything at all. Rhododendron seed is sensitive to light, and if the seed is buried you will get little or no germination. Keep the mix moist without being too wet.

There could be a problem, however, as to where to put the pots as newly germinated seeds are likely to be eaten by mice, woodlice, or slugs. My solution to this is to construct a wire-mesh table without legs. Suspend this table from the ceiling or the roof using strong wires and then the creepy crawlies have no means of access to your seedlings. By constructing it with wire mesh, you will have perfect drainage.

R. macabeanum seedpods.

Generally rhododendron seed germinates within two to four weeks. Naturally you need to keep an eye on the pots and the seedlings to make sure they stay moist, and to prevent overcrowding. When the seedlings are big enough you can prick them out, remembering to label each batch of plants.

As I write this I have small pots of tiny seedling *R. yuefengense* and *R. nuttallii* from Vietnam on my nearby shady windowsill.

CUTTINGS

Some of the big-leafs can be grown from cuttings but they can be difficult. It's not that they won't root, it's just that the stems and leaves are so unwieldy it's hard to even make cuttings, let alone keep them in good condition. The main hindrance is that the leaves are so big that even when cut back, they are still huge.

Cuttings can be taken in late spring or autumn. Late spring is probably the best time, just after the new season's growth has firmed up, when the new leaves are almost as hard and firm as the old leaves. Spring cuttings are slightly more difficult to grow because the warmer temperatures of summer may kill the cutting before it can produce roots. The advantage is that they have more vitality, and also cell activity is increased in summer and so the cutting should root faster.

Autumn cuttings, by comparison, will be much slower to root because the plant will be semi-dormant through winter. The advantage is that the cutting can survive for longer without any roots to sustain it.

Rhododendron cuttings set up under a misting system (top) and young plants in the Pukeiti nursery (below).

Remove good healthy new growth, typically 4–6 in (10–15 cm) long. You need to reduce the amount of leaf area, cutting back to no more than one third of their original length, leaving a short tight circle of trimmed foliage.

Now you need to attend to the base of the stem. Turn the cutting around and trim the stem length to 3–4 in (7–10 cm). Then remove two slivers of bark on opposite sides of the stem, right at the base, creating two shapes to look like Gothic church windows.

Dip the base of the cutting into a strong hormone mix, typically 2% IBA (indole butyric acid). Next fill a pot with very free-draining potting mix. The key thing to remember is plant roots need air as much as water and so the mix should retain moisture but have sufficient air for the cutting to survive and produce roots.

Use a pencil to make holes for the cuttings to fit into and push them in far enough so they stand up on their own. Ideally, the pots of cuttings should go into what's called a 'mist system', where a fine coating of mist sprays onto the leaves every fifteen minutes or so. This keeps the leaves fresh and turgid. In a perfect system there will be some form of heating at the base of the cuttings, at around 70°F or 20°C. The heat at the base encourages activity and cell division, so hopefully the cutting will grow roots. Meanwhile the misted tops will be in suspended animation because of the cool temperatures, and this will prevent new shoot or leaf growth. You want the cutting to put all its energy into growing roots rather than growing new leaves at this stage.

If you do not have a state of the art mist system, you can create a good substitute in a home situation. Place one, two or three cuttings in a pot of very free-draining mix. Cover the cuttings and the top of the pot with a clear plastic bag and tie the base to keep the air in the bag and to maintain a very high humidity. Because the cutting is removed from the parent plant, it will quickly dry out and wilt without high humidity. Another possibility to use as a cover over the cuttings is a large clear plastic drink bottle. Turn the empty bottle upside down, remove the base, then cut off the top with scissors or secateurs to give you a perfect dome of clear plastic. To fit big cutting material inside a confined space, you may have to drastically reduce the leaf area.

Water the cuttings well before you place the plastic cover over them. This liquid will recirculate ad infinitum within its own enclosed environment. From time to time, take the cover off to check for any disease problems. The pots of cuttings need to be in an area that is well lit without being sunny or hot. Too much sun or heat will cook them. The perfect place seems to be a bathroom windowsill with frosted windows, on the shady side of the house. Don't forget to label the cuttings with the name of the variety, the date they were made, and the source.

Many of the large-leaf group of rhododendrons, however, are difficult to root from cuttings and will need to be layered or grafted.

LAYERING

Layering is the simpler of the two techniques. The first and only real problem with layering is you need to own or have access to a plant you wish to propagate. Simple layering is the best and easiest method of propagating any shrub considered too difficult to do from cuttings. The only drawback is you need a number of stems near to ground level which can be manoeuvred into position plus some low-swooping branches touching the soil. Some people go to a lot of trouble to nick or wound the branch, and then use pegs to hold it down. The easier method by far is to place a brick on top of the stem. The brick holds the stem in place, touching the ground, and the moist humid environment under the brick encourages the stem to create new roots. You can check on progress every month or so by carefully holding the stem in place and gently lifting the brick.

Typically the new plant will have created its own roots within one growing season. When there are sufficient roots to maintain the plant, remove the stem from the mother tree and mollycoddle it for a few months until it is well established on its own roots. Keep the potted plant in a propagation area where you can check it daily for any problems.

If your mother tree has no stems near ground level, then an alternative method is air layering. Choose the spot where you want roots to grow along the stem and make a slight upward cut with a knife into the stem; perhaps up to one third of the way through. Try not to cut too far because you will weaken the stem. Place a small twig or a match in this upper cut to prevent it healing. Next you need some plastic sheeting, a handful of moist sphagnum moss and string. Wrap moist sphagnum around the cut, then wrap the plastic around that and tie it at both narrow ends so it looks like a Christmas cracker. You now have an enclosed pocket of moist humid moss and a wound that cannot easily heal, and hopefully the stem will produce new roots within. Air layering also takes one whole season or summer to succeed and you can untie one end occasionally to have a peep.

GRAFTING

Grafting is a method of propagating by attaching a scion or variety we want to grow onto an existing rootstock, plant or cutting. In other words, the scion is the plant we want to grow, and we're attaching it to an existing plant with roots. This method of propagation created a devastating problem in Britain because, in the past, the rootstock for rhododendrons was typically *R. ponticum*. Nurserymen used *R. ponticum* knowing it was an easy plant to grow,

and termed a 'good doer'. Over time, many of the scion plants died, but the roots lived on. Now *R. ponticum* is a plague in parts of Britain because it can self-layer, sucker and also spread by seed.

So before you choose your rootstock, have a care as to what this plant may do in future. The ideal rootstock should be easy to root, and a 'good doer', a robust easy-care plant. My own personal favourite is the cultivar 'Mrs J.P. Lade' suggested to me many years ago by a marvellous rhododendron man, George Swan. 'Mrs Lade' is easy to root, easy to grow and has nice clean stems to allow simple grafting. What's more, it's tough and not prone to root disease — a very important factor for a rootstock.

Of course, for our chosen big-leaf rhododendrons, the best rootstock would be a Grandia or Falconera seedling with a stem thick enough to take the graft. Because the series of these two are very closely related, any one of them should easily unite with another. The other advantage is big-leaf seedlings are more likely to be compatible for size of stem as well as genetically.

Some people use side or saddle-grafting but I think the easiest and most reliable method is cleft-grafting. Take a potted rootstock plant and snip off the top, leaving a full circle of leaves below the cut.

Next make a vertical cut straight down the cut stem on the rootstock; you are splitting the stem into two equal halves, like splitting a log of firewood. Noting how long the cut on your

Preparing scions and stock for grafting (top and bottom).

rootstock is, now make two cuts on the base of the scion the same length. Each cut should be from the bark tapering to the centre, so the two cuts meet to create a perfect wedge. These two equal cuts give two perfect slopes, meeting at a sharp point (see photo above).

Slide this wedge down into the cut on the rootstock until the four surfaces marry perfectly. Then bind the whole graft with raffia or tape. Ideally all four cut surfaces should be the same size so you can match up the cambium layers. The cambium is the active part of the stem, just below the bark, and this is where cell division, or differentiation, takes place. The problem with big-leaf rhododendrons is they have such enormous stems, you are unlikely to find a rootstock with a thick enough stem to match them. In this situation you have to marry the cambium layers on one side only. This way four layers of cambium will match up, whereas in a perfect world it should be eight.

The top of the scion should have the leaf area reduced so the scion doesn't lose too much moisture. Usually this is done after grafting in case there's any damage to the scion during the process. In the case of big-leafs, however, you will need to drastically reduce the leaf area at the beginning of the process to make the scion more manageable. Then tidy up the leaves with extra trimming afterwards.

Having completed the graft and tied it together, you should place the completed amalgam in a propagation tent, or under a plastic bottle or somewhere with high humidity to keep the scion alive. Ideally keep them cool, moist without being too wet and shaded from hot sun. Check the tie from time to time, and keep an eye on the health and hygiene. When it is obvious that the scion has united and there is visible new tissue or callus, then you can cut the tie.

The following winter when you are confident the grafted plant is a success, you can plant it in a nursery to be grown on, or plant it in its final position in the garden if you have a suitable location. Some people say you should plant at the same level as before, and this is traditional with all trees and shrubs. However, some gardeners suggest the graft is only temporary and call it a 'nurse graft' and recommend that you bury the graft so the scion can in time put out its own roots and become independent of the rootstock. My own take on this is to bury the plant slightly deeper but only cover the graft in very open compost or potting mix, allowing air to reach the stem and reduce the risk of collar rot. In time, as the scion puts out roots, then you can mulch higher and higher to allow these new roots to establish.

Above: Scions grafted onto stock before binding (left) and after binding (right).

Left: Natural seedling growing at Pukeiti.

CHAPTER 10

Placement and companion plants

PLACEMENT

Having bought or acquired your new rhododendrons, you want them to thrive. Plants are one of the few purchases in life to increase in value year by year, rather than depreciate as cars do the moment you leave the showroom. We need shade and shelter for rhododendrons and especially so for our chosen big-leaf versions. So when selecting a site for them, bear in mind the need for shade, shelter, and protection from hot sun or cold frosty weather. Likewise, consider the soil aspects and whether the site will be too wet or too dry. Direct sunlight for hours on end can dehydrate and even burn the leaves of many species; freezing temperatures can turn the plant to mush. A site with big overhead trees is less likely to suffer problems in either regard.

Soil requirements can be just as exacting, as rhododendrons need acid soil and abhor limey soils except in the wild. They also insist on free-draining soil in cultivation, though again they seem to cope with this in many wild settings.

Having satisfied all those essential requirements, it's time to look at the aesthetics. Big-leaf rhododendrons are impressive wherever you place them, but a bit of forethought at planting time can enhance your appreciation of them over the next twenty or thirty years and beyond. If the land in your garden or chosen site is flat, then you have limited choices but there are still a few to consider. Bearing in mind the flowers are only with us for a month, it's the leaves we are primarily interested in. In fact, any gardener worth their salt would happily grow these plants even if they never flowered at all, so try to find a spot where the leaves will show themselves to their greatest potential. A dark green backdrop such as provided by conifers or camellias can highlight their magnificent leaves and show them off to best effect. Also consider the height of the backdrop because when the plants are tall and in flower you may be looking up at the sun, peering to even see the rhododendron flowers.

Opposite: Hydrangeas in a woodland setting.

Now if you have sloping terrain, the possibilities are much more exciting. First question is, do we want to look down on them or up at them to admire the woolly indumentum beneath. While the indumentum on many species is exciting it's rarely as dramatic as the leaf surfaces and so you may choose to plant just one or two up on a bank where the indumentum can be seen from below: in fact, most gardeners would prefer to look down on them to fully appreciate their glorious leaves. Planting them beneath a hill track or deck provides a platform from which you can enjoy the view below with the added advantage that the flowers will be seen against a dark backdrop rather than the bright sky.

In some ways it also depends on how many you have to plant. If you have a batch of seedlings it may be interesting to plant them in all sorts of locations to establish the best site for their health and for different viewing sites.

Another factor easily overlooked is the eventual size of these big-leaf trees. While it might take years, they will eventually be huge. Having a dramatic plant hemmed in on all sides is going to greatly diminish its appeal. Imagine how wide the plant will grow, then double that figure and you might be close to its width after two or three decades, and it will still get bigger. Rhododendrons can be shifted at any size, but there is the problem of weight and size. Moving a 6-ft (2-m) high plant is easy but shifting a 20 x 20-ft (6 x 6-m) monster is going to take some serious labour — far better to get your distances right at the beginning. The easy way around the problem is to surround the choice plants with temporary or 'nurse' plants. These are plants which can be easily shifted at a later date or even grubbed out. Hydrangeas would be a good example. While beautiful in their own right, they are easy to propagate and easily replaced.

When planting my own garden from ten acres of bare paddock, I had a system of grading the plants: A was the prime, B were very good and C were expendable. I planted an A, then C, then B, another C then a choice A again. That's A C B C A. After a few years the C plants come out to give the A and Bs more space and light. Then eventually the Bs come out as well. This magical forward-planning works well until a storm destroys your best plants. But there's no harm in planning to be good even if nature has her own way in the end.

R. 'Geoff Broker'.

COMPANION PLANTS

When we think of companion plants we generally think of comparable or similar-sized plants but with rhododendrons we have to start with the trees needed to give them the protection and shade and shelter they require. In general, deciduous trees are best because they give maximum shade in summer and then allow more sunlight through during the cooler months of winter.

TREES

As we know, the big-leaf rhododendrons need high shade from trees to perform at their best. If you have old established trees, then that's fine. Ideally a mixed oak and pine canopy is best, but not every garden is blessed with such a thing. Of the deciduous trees, oaks and ash are as good as any. Ash trees can be messy as they continually drop branches and twigs, but the advantage of these trees is they are deep rooting and don't compete too strongly with the shrubs below.

A paulownia in full flower.

If you're starting from bare ground you may want something faster growing to give 'instant' shelter. Two trees capable of growing phenomenally fast are poplars and paulownias. Poplars are not too greedy and grow very fast. They are prone to breaking during heavy winds especially when the trees are young, but they get stronger as they older.

Poplars are easily grown by sawing large branches from an existing tree and planting the bottom third of the stem or post into the ground. As a generalisation, the bigger the log the faster your tree will grow. Ideally, plant the logs the same day as you cut them as they may struggle to survive if they dry out. Some people choose broomstick-size stems and use a crowbar to plant them. It depends on your workload and how many you have to plant.

In warmer climes, a very fast-growing tree is the paulownia with their big floppy leaves. These massive leaves give instant shade to any rhododendrons or shrub beneath. They can grow 10–15 ft (3–4.5 m) in the first year and often 4–6 ft (1–2 m) a year in subsequent summers. The advantage of paulownias is that while they have some big searching roots, they do not have a mass of roots near the surface competing for moisture and nutrients. They've been used to perfection in this role at the world class Shamrock Hydrangea collection in Varengeville sur Mer near Dieppe in France. Catalpa trees, with their similar heart-shaped leaves, may work but they are a bit messy and rather brittle.

Melia azedarach is another warm-climate possibility because it grows fast and creates wonderful shade with its diverse leaf pattern. It has a tidy, wide-spreading habit but they may not be tall enough for mature big-leaf rhododendrons. However, they would be ideal for establishing smaller specimens, and then cut out when your rhododendrons mature. This tree has a huge advantage in coastal regions because it is salt- and wind-tolerant, but is despised in some warmer regions, like Georgia, USA, where it has established as a weed.

There are numerous fast-growing tall deciduous trees to choose from such as *Liriodendron* and *Liquidambar*, though both are brittle in strong winds. *Nyssa* is another possibility. In all three cases there are American and Chinese versions, all with their good points.

Magnolia delavayi at the Church Garden, New Zealand (top) and *Cornus florida* at Hackfalls Arboretum, New Zealand (bottom).

If you are blessed with a mild climate and not too much wind, then deciduous magnolias would be a great choice for a canopy tree. Their big bold leaves create enough shade, they grow fast and have the fantastic bonus of masses of blooms in early spring. Picture the combination of huge chalice-like magnolia flowers and a mass of vibrant rhododendrons beneath. If you suffer frequent frosts, then choose the later-flowering varieties with the aim of avoiding frost damage. Magnolias are perfect in terms of the health of the rhododendrons beneath because they have wiry, searching roots growing deep into the ground. Therefore these roots do not compete with the surface-rooting rhododendrons. Some gardeners feel they create too much shade, but it depends on how close they are situated in relation to the rhododendrons. Perhaps plant them so they shade the bushes from the mid-afternoon sun, rather than directly overhead.

Another possibility if you have a mild climate is to grow *Magnolia delavayi* among your giant rhododendrons, which is more of a mirror image than a tall shade provider. This wonderful evergreen magnolia with magnificent leaves would be the perfect blend with our chosen giants. The pink-flowered form from the Kunming region of Yunnan has slimmer darker leaves and would be the better choice. Even the overall domed outline of the plant would sit well with round-top rhododendrons. *Magnolia grandiflora* is another possibility, but the very shiny leaves would make your rhododendrons look dull.

Willows and birches are rather greedy and take all the moisture and goodness from the soil, depleting the nutrients your rhododendrons need, but pines are another possibility. Some gardens are blessed with big pine trees and they provide reasonable shade if their trunks are at a distance: too close and the greedy roots and the toxic needles can suppress your rhododendrons. They are good in moderation, say in a mixed woodland. Pines are more of a problem when planted en masse as they create too much shade, rob the soil, as well as poison the ground with their needles.

If you want similar-sized plants to match your giant rhododendrons then you could choose some of the following deciduous small trees with a dome shape. There are a few small deciduous trees such as *Stuartia sinensis* and *S. koreana*, as well as *Styrax japonica* with that neat domed effect. *Oxydendrum arboreum*, *Picrasma quassioides* and *Pistacia chinensis* are all possibilities.

Cornus florida from the Appalachians is a perfect complement to rhododendrons if they suit your climate. The tree casts light shade and is the perfect small tree for a mixed woodland dell, decked with glorious bract-like flowers in the spring. The colours range from white through various shades of pink. They are often hard to grow in a soft climate like Britain without the necessary baking summers and cold winters, plus various debilitating diseases attack them in some regions. In this case, the name *florida* means beautiful rather than hailing from the state of Florida. In contrast, and perhaps somewhat ironically, another plant called *Illicium floridanum*, an underrated hardy shrub with red-wine flowers, does in fact come from Florida, as indicated by the epithet *floridanum*. And from the west coast of USA comes *Cornus nuttallii* which is worth considering as a larger shade-giving tree with showy-white flowers.

Opposite: Magnolia 'Vulcan' at the Jury Garden, New Zealand.

Cryptomeria japonica trees to the rear of the garden at Pukeiti. The cherry in flower at the left is *Prunus* x *yedoensis* and the azalea at front is 'Only One Earth'.

Cherries have that same dome shape but somehow they are too formal — too urban, whereas our big-leafs should help us visualise the distant Himalayas. In California and on up the west coast of America it would be sensible to make use of native trees such as the unpopular but useful *Myrica californica*, the showy *Arbutus menziesii* and the aforementioned *Cornus nuttallii*. On the east coast of America it would be sensible to use the native *Liquidambar*, *Liriodendron* and *Magnolia fraseri*. In Britain, the obvious choices are the native oaks, pines and ash.

Some trees would be fine in terms of their overhead leaf cover but their roots are too greedy and so they diminish the strength of your prized plants below. Trees such as eucalyptus are especially greedy; elms are in this same category, and they tend to sucker as well. English beech is so dominant few other plants can survive beneath them. Even pines, larches and Douglas fir, which look perfect, can be too dominant and overly competitive, although fine at a distance where their needles and branches provide shade, but the roots are not close enough to have an impact.

Tsuga species are ideal for creating dappled shade for all rhododendrons. Different *Tsuga* or hemlock seem to occur on the high passes of so many countries, for example, in America, Japan, Korea, China, Bhutan and Nepal. In the Himalayas, they are often seen in tandem with big-leaf rhododendrons, so if you plant a group of *Tsuga* you are creating exactly the situation the big-leaf plants enjoy in the wild. *Tsuga* can be fast or slow-growing depending on the situation; too warm, and they sulk, but in a cool moist climate they can romp away.

Another fine conifer is the *Cryptomeria japonica* from Japan. Most gardeners in the northern hemisphere are more familiar with the fluffy juvenile form with the pleasing habit of changing from green to bronze in winter time. They can stay in juvenile mode for fifty years or more and become a tree in their own right. The adult form, with thick cord-like foliage, is the better tree for an arboretum. As a young plant it has a perfect conical habit, later becoming a wide-topped tree, as old conifers do. As a part of a mixed woodland, it's a terrific tree but as with any conifer species, too many of them and they take all the light, moisture and nutrients. Another advantageous feature is the ability of this seemingly soft-wooded tree to withstand wind: regular gales make no impression on them and they even tolerate hurricanes.

Coastal redwood, *Sequoia sempervirens*, has similar attributes to the *Cryptomeria*, being a tall dense conifer which is ideal in moderation but a plantation of them will smother everything beneath. Both are fast-growing trees and tolerate coastal gales.

Walnuts of any description are an anathema as they exude chemicals which depress the growth of any nearby plants, sweet chestnuts cast too much shade with their dense canopy of hand-sized leaves and alders can be too greedy with their aggressive roots and overly dominant canopy of foliage.

SHRUBS

Big-leaf rhododendrons, especially the Grandia and Falconera series, are so big and so majestic it can be hard to find suitable shrubs to blend with them. Any shrubs with thin wispy leaves look pathetic next to the magnificent rhododendron foliage. Even typical rhododendrons are overshadowed by them, but they can be used in moderation. It depends how many big-leaf plants you have. If there are groves of them then you need to be specific and choose a few equally majestic plants. On the other hand, if you have just one or two big-leaf rhododendrons then more general, mixed garden plants are quite feasible. Typical woodland garden plants such as *Pieris*, camellias, azaleas and *Corylopsis* all look good.

The moist mild climate needed for big-leaf rhododendrons is also ideally suited to a range of evergreen and somewhat tender South American shrubs. *Crinodendron hookerianum* with its spear-like black-green leaves makes a handsome pillar, but when it flowers, everyone wants one. Fat cherry-like red lanterns decorate the bush and turn it into something magical. There is one other species, *Crinodendron patagua*, but it doesn't rate by comparison, forming a small plum-like tree with white bell flowers.

Pieris formosa var. *forrestii* at Gwavas Garden, New Zealand.

Embothrium coccineum is slightly easier to grow and will thrill you with a mass of hot orange-red tubular flowers in springtime, generally coinciding with mid-season big-leaf rhododendrons. The bush is always upright in habit, though not always a tidy pillar. Being so tall with a weak root system, they are prone to wind-throw. Often the plant has a tendency to sucker and you could encourage this by scarring some of the surface roots. When the bush grows as a thicket of stems it becomes so much more wind-resistant, as each trunk acts as a guy rope to the others. The finger-sized dark green leaves look good all year.

Eucryphia is a fine genus found naturally in Chile, Australia and Tasmania. All are evergreen, or almost so, and all have an upright almost column habit. Most flower late spring or early summer, thus extending the overall flowering season. *E. cordifolia* from Chile has wavy, grey leaves and masses of white flowers reminiscent of a buttercup flower. *E. lucida* from Tasmania is a tidy upright bush with narrow waxy greyish leaves and small white or pink flowers depending on the clone. From south-east Australia is the fine *E. moorei* with greyish pinnate leaves and a mass of white flowers in mid-summer.

The hybrid forms of *E.* x *nymansensis* are more at home in the northern hemisphere. There are two basic types: those favouring the greyish foliage of *E. cordifolia* such as the clone 'Mount Usher'; and those more like *E. glutinosa* with glossy green mostly trifoliate foliage seen in the clone 'Nymansay'. Both forms have the ability to produce different foliage on the same bush.

Azara from Chile and Argentina are worth considering. *A. microphylla* has tiny almost black leaves, and tiny fluffy yellow flowers with a scent like vanilla. The bush is very upright and tidy, creating a column of foliage. By contrast *A. serrata* has bright grass-green leaves decked with brilliant balls of buttercup yellow flowers. The other species all have scented yellowish flowers but can't compete for beauty of foliage.

For a large collection of big-leafs you need more dramatic plantings such as hydrangeas with their big leaves. They have the added benefit of extending your season by flowering in the summer when the rhododendrons display foliage only. Effectively this gives you two major flowering seasons in one calendar year. A major advantage of using hydrangeas is they are easy to propagate and therefore a cheap, or free, plant. As your rhododendrons grow bigger they will overshadow and even kill the shrubs beneath, but you can plant a fresh batch of hydrangea cuttings near the drip line.

When we talk hydrangeas, most people think of the *H. macrophylla* types but some of the other species are perhaps more suited to blend with big-leaf rhododendrons. There have been many forms of *H. aspera* coming out of the Himalayas in recent years. Whereas the typical *H. aspera* ssp. *villosa* has fairly small narrow leaves, there are new forms with leaves bigger than dinner plates. Most are surprisingly hardy coming as they do from the same regions and even the same forests as the big-leaf rhododendrons. In Bhutan, we saw hydrangea trees capable of holding six very large langur monkeys teasing a leaping aggressive dog.

Smaller species of hydrangeas, such as *H. scandens chinensis* and *H. serrata*, with their lace-cap flowers, seem to blend well with rhododendrons.

Lindera obtusiloba at Gwavas Garden, New Zealand.

If you want something exotic, you could go for *Trochodendron aralioides* with its dramatic palmate foliage, and some of the New Zealand *Pseudopanax* would create a similar effect with their stunning foliage and a rounded bush shape similar to a camellia. Camellia species are another possibility although their immaculate upright column habit does jar or clash with the round-topped rhododendrons.

If you want dramatic and unusual foliage, it might be worth seeking out plants such as *Salix magnifica* with blue-toned magnolia-likes leaves, or perhaps the beautiful *Lindera obtusiloba* with striking three-lobed leaves turning a beautiful gold in the autumn or fall. *Daphniphyllum macropodum* looks exotic and has rhododendron-like leaves and is incredibly cold-hardy as it hails from Korea. Some forms have attractive red petioles, and the bush looks glorious every day of the year. Most plants tend to have an off-season.

Stalwarts such as *Pieris* are worth considering as they look good all year and present us with three different coats depending on the season — neat tidy shiny leaves dress the plant for most of the year, changing to hot-pink or red new foliage in the spring, plus a show of dainty white bells. Like *Pieris, Kalmia latifolia* is another acid-loving member of the

Ericaceae family. Kalmias tolerate extreme cold and cope with some shade though they will grow in full sun too. Some gardeners find them a challenge to grow. A somewhat neglected plant in the same family is the perfect ground cover in a woodland situation. *Leucothoe fontanesiana* has rich green arrow-like leaves which look good all through the year. It's one of those plants with a sense of direction and invariable the arching stems and leaves all face one way. If you have a slight slope or bank, it looks terrific all weeping en masse. Sometimes in chilly winters the leaves take on a reddish hue. The white spikes of flowers are somewhat like a *Pieris* but not as showy.

If you have a warmer climate you might be tempted to try big succulent leaves of the giant *Senecio* — *S. petasites* and *S. grandifolius* syn. *Telanthophora grandifolia*. The big *Brugmansia* or *Datura* are lush leafy shrubs with grand foliage but too tender for most regions. In an Australian or New Zealand setting, a backdrop of native bush forest is ideal as it blends perfectly with rhododendrons; it's as if they were meant to be together.

Still with exotics, there is a range of tree ferns which add a touch of the tropics to the scene. While not strictly trees in the accepted sense, they can grow to 40–50 ft (12–15 m). The *Cyathea* are the giants and generally more tender, but even some of these will tolerate snow in their homeland. Perhaps more practical for northern hemisphere gardeners are the stouter hardier *Dicksonia* with their rough, hard fronds. The hardiest species seems to be *D. antarctica* from Tasmania and southern Australia. The two New Zealand species cope with snow and severe frosts in their homeland but don't always cope when transported to the northern hemisphere. *D. squarrosa* has thin spiky trunks and the more robust *D. fibrosa* has an enormously thick trunk and a handsome skirt of old fronds beneath the canopy of new fronds. *Dicksonia* grow perfectly perpendicular and tend to be slower growing, shorter squat plants whereas the more exotic *Cyathea* grow taller and more wayward.

PERENNIALS AND GROUND-COVER PLANTS

Hostas and bluebells at Pukeiti.

Traditionally in a woodland garden, you would expect to find plants such as primulas, lilies, evergreen iris and *Meconopsis*. With ground covers you can go big or small. Big leaves mirror the rhododendrons and thus create a picture where everything is in balance, but in a dell with primarily big-leaf rhododendrons, it looks more in keeping if you choose other large-leaf plants such as *Hosta* and *Ligularia* for the ground cover.

Hosta come in a range of colours including many variegated types. Although it's a matter of taste and choice, most purists would probably go for the simple soft lettuce-green of *Hosta plantaginea* 'Grandiflora', or solid greys and blues like *H. sieboldiana*, or *H. tokudama*. All are happy in shade but will tolerate sunshine if they receive enough rainfall and have a mulch to keep the roots cool and moist. Single-colour *Hosta* are much more tolerant of sun than the variegated types. *Hosta* are remarkable plants for suppressing weeds. Naturally the dense leaf cover in summer shades out the weeds and prevents new seedlings germinating because there is no light. But even in winter time, when there are no leaves on the *Hosta*, the dense root mass seems to be enough to inhibit any weeds.

PLACEMENT AND COMPANION PLANTS

Glyn Church sheltering under a *Gunnera chilensis* growing in his garden in Taranaki, New Zealand.

Ligularia are fantastic ground cover, providing a dense, even layer of foliage and do a terrific job of suppressing weeds. Most have big round leaves in shades of green, grey and reddy-bronze, and show their true colours in autumn or even winter when they produce yellow or orange daisy flowers. Most never become weedy, though the *L. dentata* 'Desdemona' does self-seed, producing a range of leaf colours from straight green through to bronze. This plant is deciduous, whereas many of the *Ligularia* are evergreen and look equally good all through winter. *Ligularia* tolerate shade or sunshine except for the very large-leaf *Farfugium japonicum* 'Giganteum' (often sold as *Ligularia reniformis*) which tends to wilt in hot sun. But in a shady situation these giant kidney-shaped leaves are glorious and may even outshine your giant rhododendrons with huge bright glossy green leaves.

Still with big bold leaves, there is the moist-loving *Darmera peltata*, better known perhaps as *Peltiphyllum peltata,* with crinkle-cut rounded leaves and tall spikes of pink flowers in the spring. It's a deciduous plant, as is the slightly similar *Podophyllum* genus. These Asian and American deciduous ground covers have leaves vaguely like a maple, often spectacularly variegated with brown and marbled colours and cute, nodding flowers in the spring.

As a bold ground cover, *Bergenia* are hard to beat. Their waxy plate-like leaves look good all year and the bright pink spring flowers are a bonus. Happy in shade, they cope with just about any soil or situation.

But if you want truly bold leaves then you can't ignore the giant Chilean *Gunnera chilensis*. These massive umbrella-like leaves will protect you from any storm if you can brave the semi-hard spikes along the petiole and beneath the leaf. Huge crowns develop if the plant is given enough moisture to sustain it. It's certainly an impact plant with leaves a metre wide. As you might imagine, the flowers cones are equally impressive growing from ground level to knee high, though the actual flowers are minuscule.

For ground covers it's possible, however, to go small and still look good, perhaps because of the big contrast of leaf size. A large drift of self-sown forget-me-nots (*Myosotis arvensis*) is hard to beat. They create a froth of pale blue flowers to coincide with mainstream rhododendrons. Once established, the weeds seem to let them have free rein and don't try to compete. They produce so many seedlings the cover gets thicker and thicker every year. A great advantage is the way they self-seed, so as your giant rhododendrons shade them out of one zone they will colonise new ground.

Another possibility is the related *Omphalodes cappadocica* with charming blue flowers. This plant looks tidy all year with its spathe-like leaves. In the same borage family, the twin-coloured *Symphytum* with pink and blue flowers is a possibility though they do tend to be a cultivated garden plant rather than a woodland dell one.

A classy genus of ground-cover plants is *Epimedium* sp. The triangular or rounded leaves are bronzy or red when they first emerge in spring, softening to shades of green. They take a while to establish but eventually create a dense mat capable of suppressing weeds. Find the time to trim off any dead or dying leaves in winter to leave the scene clear and clean for the small starry flowers to show off in the spring.

Perhaps you could also try primulas, but in general they need more moisture and light than they are likely to get under your big-leafs. Ferns are another possibility, especially the tidy shuttlecock ferns such as *Osmunda*, *Blechnum* and *Dryopteris*. A large drift of shuttlecocks is very impressive in a woodland hollow.

Another possibility is to plant drifts of creeping iris such as *Iris evansia*, *I. wattii* or similar. These plants are better off with some shade and will tolerate heavy shade. Less tolerant of shade but still a good match in terms of boldness are the *Hemerocallis* or daylilies.

You can of course plant true lilies to match the grandeur of your big-leafs. Plant them in the vicinity but not directly under the plants as the fibrous rhododendron roots will suppress the lily bulbs. One lily that looks incredible when grown with rhododendrons is the giant *Cardiocrinum giganteum*. The glorious heart-shaped leaves sit in a tidy pirouette before extending to produce a magnificent flower spike 10 ft (3 m) tall. The leaves are lettuce green and very shiny and the huge white trumpets have a rich red-maroon centre. Just to top it all off, the flowers are deliciously scented. The only problem is, having 'sold' them to you, I have to confess they are extremely hard to grow, although if they do decide they like you, they are likely to become a weed. It's a bit like mint — you either have too much or none at all. In general, they like a cool high-rainfall climate but I have seen them thrive in some dry gardens.

Other bulbs such as bluebells, trilliums and dog's tooth violets (*Erythronium dens-canis*), or autumn crocus (*Colchicum autumnale*) will look pretty and add a touch of colour in a different season.

One thing you must bear in mind when planting bulbs and ground covers under these massive-leaf giants is the equally giant-leaf litter and the way these big-leafs take all the light from above. An established plant will have such a dense layer of leaf litter, no little ground-cover plant is going to cope with the lack of light and deposits from above. Add to this the shade created by the canopy of leaves and most little ground covers are going to fade away.

Cardiocrinum giganteum growing among big-leaf rhododendrons at Pukeiti.

CHAPTER 11

Conservation—what we can do to save the giant rhododendrons from extinction

One of the factors in favour of rhododendrons thriving in the wild is they grow in remote regions of the world where few people want to live. Cold wet mountain tops are not ideal for farming and any cultivation and so the rhododendrons are often left alone. With poor roads logging is often not an option and this helps their cause. The biggest threat is from cutting for firewood. Even here, there is a sunny aspect to this because most rhododendrons do not die if chopped down but simply regenerate. Even if the forest is burnt, rhododendrons tend to spring back to life after the event

Another bonus is they often grow on precipitous cliffs which are difficult if not impossible to traverse. Be it plant or animal, for most species, the further they live from civilisation, the better their chance of survival. Many species have a wide distribution and this diversification is wonderful because if one colony is wiped out, others will continue. (Generally speaking, the wider the distribution of plants or animals across the globe, the greater the genetic diversification and the ability to adapt is likely to be.) But in the case of the big-leafs it seems quite a few species grow on just one mountain slope and nowhere else in the world: several new species have been discovered in the last twenty years growing in remote mountain eyries.

Above: *R. protistum*, western China and Myanmar.

Opposite: *R. macabeanum*, collected in the wild by Thomson and Dayal from Mt Japfu, Nagaland, north-east India.

Regenerating large-leaf rhododendrons in *Abies* forest, Bhutan.

But for all those good points listed above, in the last hundred years, since George Forrest discovered the magnificent giant *R. protistum* var. *giganteum*, the number of big-leaf rhododendrons in the wild has greatly diminished. This is mostly due to pressure on land in the Himalayas as local human populations swell.

In economically poor highland countries the main source of fuel is local timber and as it happens, rhododendron wood burns particularly well and is very useful for heating and for cooking as it's a dense heavy wood that burns efficiently, and will also burn green. Most timbers need to be stored and dried before they can be burnt. Because of the qualities of instant heat and efficiency, the rhododendron is the most common timber used for fuel and firewood.

Compared to other timbers it gives off lots of heat and is as good as ash, cherry or members of the Myrtaceae family such as eucalyptus. The question is what alternative wood is available for heating and cooking other than cutting down ancient rhododendrons? Well the aforementioned eucalyptus is one possibility. The drawback is that gum trees have a tendency to ruin the soil because they are so greedy, and thus it is often difficult to grow other plants nearby. In places like Portugal, they have found cropping gum trees ruins the soil and sours it for any future crops.

For the farmers, the problem is that greedy gum tree roots rob the soil of any goodness and moisture, as well as depositing a thick carpet of waxy leaves which never seem to rot down. Instead of providing an organic mulch as say a layer of oak leaves, these gum leaves, full of tannins and oils, will sour the soil. Another long-term problem with gums is that they self-seed and eventually gum tree forests could dominate these hillsides.

There are alternatives: the Australian wattles or acacias work well as fast-growing firewood trees but they too can also self-seed prolifically. The advantage of both gum and wattle is the phenomenal speed of growth, creating firewood in as little as ten years compared to decades for traditional firewood species.

Perhaps a better alternative is to use existing species from the region such as *Alnus nepalensis*, a very fast-growing species capable of supplying some firewood within five to ten years from seed. A bonus is the tree has nitrogen-fixing nodules on the roots similar to legumes and this allows the tree to grow on poor soils as it can access atmospheric nitrogen to feed the plant and this, plus leaf deposit, eventually makes the soil richer.

This fast-growing alder species has other winning attributes. It grows over a huge altitudinal range and has big potential because it will grow on difficult sites, or areas considered worthless to farmers. It will grow all across the Himalayas on dry rocky sites, soggy wet ground, or on impoverished terraces abandoned by farmers. Unfortunately the timber from the tree is poor quality other than as firewood, or perhaps as piles for houses in wet areas.

But just as we need the whole forest to preserve the rhododendrons, the locals have other uses for the forest trees. Timber is needed by locals to build houses and barns. The really tall *Tsuga* species are pit-sawn for the straight-grained strong timber it produces. In a tough environment, nothing is wasted and the brush is used for animal bedding and for firewood.

Pine timber varies in strength and lasting qualities. In Nepal they use the blue pine, *Pinus wallichiana*, for making lintels, beams and doorposts. The timber is adzed to create the shape needed. Blue pine is exceptionally hard and dense, and also full of resin. It is almost impossible to split into firewood, but these other qualities give it higher status and value. Another conifer, the *Taxus* or yew also provides good building timber.

Betula utilis grows across the Himalayas and are often observed as the last trees, growing at the highest points before the climate reduces everything to scrub. *Betula* is good firewood and the bark is sometimes used to exclude the damp under the eaves of houses in places like Nepal. In high population areas, the brush from the trees is used for animal fodder. A common sight is to see many tree species limbed up by agile boys who climb up to cut off branches for fodder. This use of foliage and brush puts pressure on the forests as vast quantities are harvested for animal fodder. *Quercus semecarpifolia* is a prime target for this activity because it provides good nutrition and the plant quickly recovers from the mutilation. All oaks and the related *Castanopsis* species are used for firewood and fodder.

Tall-growing *Abies* such as *Abies spectabilis* in Nepal have a completely different use in house construction. When the trees reach a certain maturity the timber can be split to create shingles for roofing. Locals slash a blaze in the bark to test the timber for splitting qualities before felling the tree. These species could be afforded some protection if locals could be persuaded to use alternative roofing materials such as slate or roofing iron, but of course it costs money they don't have to buy it and transport is also expensive in regions with poor infrastructure.

Alternatives to firewood such as solar panels are a terrific asset at these high altitudes with high sunshine hours but again the initial cost is beyond most local people. Perhaps an aid project based on bringing in roofing iron and solar panels to poor regions of Nepal would significantly reduce pressure on the forests. It's interesting to see the Chinese make frequent use of solar panels in Yunnan and Tibet.

Other useful schemes would be to persuade people to use kerosene for cooking instead of wood. Even simple things like plastic guttering on hotels and guesthouses to collect rainwater rather than have people trekking for miles to carry water for tourists would ease the pressure on the community and the environment.

ARUNACHAL PRADESH

A small neglected part of the world which is very difficult to access because of the political situation. In addition, there are the physical difficulties of getting to a region with poor roads and much of the steep country covered in dense forest. In some ways this is good because the forests remain intact, and hopefully this is good for conservation. A fortunate side effect of globalisation is many young people want to move to the cities and so there is less pressure on the land. So currently the region is out of sight, out of mind, but the conservation situation looks good.

The government is setting up a botanical reserve in the west of the province with a strong emphasis on native rhododendrons. The idea is to have protected areas at different altitudes and enhance the flora with additional plantings of native species.

R. kesangiae growing in forest.

ASSAM, NAGALAND AND MANIPUR

In the case of Assam, its population has grown in similar fashion to Nepal, putting a huge strain on the forests. Much of the natural vegetation has been cut down over the last century. Hopefully, pressure from the Indian government will gradually lead to a better future for the local people as they become educated and learn new techniques of growing and harvesting trees for firewood to heat their homes. As the younger generation prefer to move to the cities, there will less pressure on the native forests for firewood or to clear land for cultivation.

BHUTAN

Bhutan is a special case because they already have a wonderful policy of protecting their native forests, added to which they have a very high rate of literacy and spend much of their tourist dollar on education. With education comes knowledge and the local people take pride in their environment, and they become the protectors of the forest.

Another positive step taken by the Bhutanese is the setting up of two botanical gardens: one a general garden of native species on the hills above the capital Thimpu; the other, more excitingly for rhododendron-lovers, is the establishment of a rhododendron garden with the emphasis on native rhododendrons. This unique garden is in the Thrumshingla National Park in the very centre of the country, near Trongsa.

By supporting either of these gardens you can make a significant contribution to the preservation of big-leaf rhododendrons. Bhutan has many native rhododendrons including *R. griffithii*, *R. grande*, *R. hodgsonii*, *R. falconeri* and the recently discovered *R. kesangiae*. This last was thought to be endemic to Bhutan but recent trips to Arunachal Pradesh by Steve Hootman have proved otherwise — not that this detracts from the efforts of the Bhutanese in preserving this precious plant.

Jiaozishan, north-east Yunnan, in full flower, with the gondola for easy viewing, Chinese style.

CHINA

China is perceived as the villain in the piece because they chopped down so much of their forest to make pig iron back in Chairman Mao's day, but even one hundred years ago, George Forrest noted that so much of the original forest had already been cut down, and he doubted much more would be found, except in the remotest areas where nobody lived. This was back in his early collection days so perhaps Mao's devastation was not as great as people think.

In many ways it's too late to save the big old forests. There are pockets remaining and nowadays they are making an attempt to preserve what is left. Most of the favourite habitats like the Cangshan, Laojunshan (the mountain with *R. sinofalconeri*), Zhibenshan and Jiaozishan are now controlled-access areas where plant collection policies are in place to preserve the status quo. The problem with many is that people still live within the boundaries and are reluctant to give up their lifestyles. Key local reserves are also being created to help save what is left of the woodland areas, improving the chances of survival of the indigenous forest — or what remains, even if now much modified. The largest reserve in Yunnan is the Gaoligong Mountain Nature Reserve with over 988,422 acres (400,000 hectares) with numerous vegetation types.

Taking a gondola ride up through a prime forest or alpine area may seem incongruous to us but it opens the area up to the Chinese people who would not visit if they had not had the chance. Most are town-dwellers and a day in the country is a novelty, but done with creature comforts such as this, the actual human footprint is not a major problem. For the local people, it offers a source of income that is more assured than their subsistence farming or tree-felling. Hopefully that equates to a better future for what forest is left, even if it's not as 'pristine' as what it might have been when we first visited it many years before. How 'pristine' was it another fifty years before that, one asks?

Another factor in the preservation of the forests is the shift towards electricity for cooking, rather than using fuel wood. Solar heating is also becoming more commonplace. And efforts to reduce soil erosion have also been made.

NEPAL

Nepal is a classic example of a country where the human head count has increased dramatically. Back in 1919, when Forrest discovered his rhododendron tree in Yunnan, the population in Nepal was just over 5 million. By 1950, it was around 8 million and now it's close to 30 million. The land, the forest and the environment of some of these Himalayan countries simply can't cope with such huge increases in population.

However, on the bright side, the government is continually adding to the national parks, currently encompassing around 16 per cent of the land mass. By creating a national park it makes it easier to manage and conserve the region but it's not guaranteed to protect all the plants and animals within the zone. Think of it like politicians in the West who create a traffic speed limit and somehow think we will all abide by their new rule. Likewise, the Nepalese villagers will continue their lifestyle as before. In theory, only dead trees can be harvested from a national park, but that puts more pressure on trees in the immediate vicinity of the park.

Nepali farmers not only use rhododendron wood for fuel, but also cut stems and branches to drape along fences as a deterrent to stock. The animals know rhododendron is poisonous and avoid it, thus making a weak fence stronger than it might otherwise be.

Each village is run by a committee of locals and by negotiation some areas around the village can be designated as 'no-go' areas where the forest remains intact.

R. arboreum growing with *Pinus wallichiana* in Nepal.

The problems with deforestation, however, cannot be laid solely at the door of local people. Huge numbers of tourists and trekkers put pressure on the system. Vast amounts of timber are cut, carried and burnt to provide hot water for showers for visitors who want to be squeaky clean. This is especially true in the Everest region.

Some regions have reforestation programmes but it's mostly small scale. *Pinus wallichiana* is the most commonly planted tree, plus some *P. patula* from Mexico. Mostly the planting is on dry slopes not suitable for farming, but the trees take a long time to get established in this harsh environment and only really get cracking when their tops shade the root zone.

The national parks in the north and eastern half of the country are best for rhododendrons, namely Sagarmatha National Park, Langtang National Park, Makalu Barun National Park, and Shey Phoksundo National Park.

SIKKIM

Sikkim has a low population and this means much of its forest is intact. There is not the pressure from farmers or people needing fuel in quite the same way as in Nepal. A huge percentage, nearly 50 per cent, of the state is intact natural forest with around 33 per cent under snows and alpine meadows and looking just like it did in Joseph Hooker's day.

Indiscriminate cutting of trees is illegal and generally only granted for infrastructure development such as road building and hydroelectric projects. There is no logging industry as such.

R. hodgsonii, Yumthang Valley, Sikkim.

Sikkim has a series of national parks preserving virgin forest and areas of high importance for the preservation of rare plants and animals and unique environments. National parks and wildlife sanctuaries account for around 43 per cent of the land mass as Protected Area Network.

Khangchendzonga National Park has a mountain of the same name, the third highest peak in the world at just over 28,000 ft (8500 m) and the overall size of the park is enormous, over 1784 sq miles (4620 sq km). It has further been declared a Biosphere Reserve and the entire area now stands at 1012 sq miles (2620 sq km).

The Shingba Rhododendron Sanctuary near Lachung in the north has around forty species of our favourite genus including *R. falconeri, R. grande,* and *R. hodgsonii*. And the Barsey Rhododendron Sanctuary in the west, on the Nepalese border, is part of the Singalila Range where Hooker botanised. It contains both *R. falconeri* and *R. hodgsonii*.

For lovers of giant rhododendrons, the establishment of the Kyongnosla Alpine Sanctuary, at Tsongmo Lake near Gangtok will raise their spirits. This sanctuary was established by Keshab C. Pradhan to protect big-leaf and other rhododendrons, as well as the diverse wildlife.

VIETNAM

Vietnam has a network of national parks and scenic reserves throughout the country, set up with the aim of protecting biodiversity as their primary objective. This preserves various habitats as well as the bird and plant life and, in the process, is becoming a valuable focus for tourism. While areas are officially protected, people still live in these areas, so it may not be as pristine and protected as we might like, but at least the areas are valued by the authorities.

In a more general sense you can join organisations. Following is a list of conservation organisations, including their prime aims.

World Wildlife Fund is focussed primarily on animals but also works on conservation of habitat.
www.worldwildlife.org

'Rare' is an organisation designed to work with people to engender pride in their local endangered species.
www.rare.org

R. rex ssp. fictolacteum, Meerkerk Gardens, Seattle, USA.

Roots and Shoots is part of the Jane Goodall Institute and is designed to get young people around the world involved in conservation.
www.janegoodall.org/programs/rootsandshoots/about

The Nature Conservancy is based in the USA and works to preserve plants and animals by buying up land that is home to endangered species.
www.nature.org

International Dendrology Society, headquartered in England, with branches all around the world. Primarily focussed on trees, this organisation encourages the growing of trees, especially rare trees, and helping members gain more knowledge of both cultivated and wild trees. Every year members organise tours of European gardens as well as tours of more distant lands to see native forests, gardens and tree collections. To become a member, one has to be a professional tree person or else have an arboretum or tree collection open to visitors for education and science.
www.dendrology.org

For more specific plant-related groups, or those who focus on rhododendrons or trees, there are several key association groups for rhododendrons. Their prime aim is the promotion of rhododendrons with special emphasis on encouraging members to grow rhododendrons and to increase their knowledge.

Rhododendron Species Botanical Garden PO Box 3798, Federal Way, Washington WA 98063
www.rhodygarden.org

American Rhododendron Society, P.O. Box 525, Niagara Falls, NY 14304
www.rhododendron.org
(There are Danish and Scottish chapters of the American Rhododendron Society.)

Rhododendron Society of Canada has branches in Niagara, Victoria, Vancouver, Toronto and Halifax, Nova Scotia.
www.rhodoniagara.org

Australian Rhododendron Society has branches in all the southern states.
www.rhododendron.com.au

The New Zealand Rhododendron Association has branches throughout the country.
www.rhododendron.org.nz

The Rhododendron, Camellia & Magnolia Group of the Royal Horticultural Society based in Wisley, England.
www.rhodogroup-rhs.org

Still on the subject of saving these remarkable rhododendrons from extinction, we can all do our bit by trying to grow them ourselves or, alternatively, by helping gardens around the world which specialise in these plants.

R. protistum 'Pukeiti' — Graham Smith with the original tree at Pukeiti, New Zealand.

Glossary

Clone — a selected plant from a group of the same species with outstanding attributes and often named i.e. R *montroseanum* 'Benmore'.

Cultivar — short for 'cultivated variety' which is similar to 'clone' but will be man-made by crossing two forms of the same species together.

Hybrid — a man-made cross between two different species or cultivars and given a unique name i.e. R. 'Gibraltar' ('Bibiani' x *elliottii*) – a hybrid crossed with a species.

Rhododendron — is the generic name or Genus for this large group of more than 900 individual species. The name means 'Rose Tree' in Latin.

Subsection — a subdivision of the very large Rhododendron genus, as in Falconera and Grandia.

Subspecies — (ssp.) a division of the species rank that identifies a similar group of plants but not sufficiently different to demand full specific rank, i.e. R. *rex* ssp. *fictolacteum*.

Variety — (var.) a division of the species rank that recognises variability within the same species i.e. R. *kesangiae* var. *album*.

FLOWER

Campanulate — typical shape of an individual flower like a tubular funnel or bell.
  Funnel campanulate: wide-spreading tube
  Oblique campanulate: flower held stiffly at an oblique angle
  Tubular campanulate: narrower short tube
  Ventricose campanulate: swollen side to the tube, often waxy flowers

Corolla — the whole flower, tube and lobes.

Lobes — the rounded flared ends of each tube forming the mouth, usually 7–10, occasionally 5.

Nectar pouches — sac-like hollows in the base of the corolla which often contain nectar in Grandia subsection.

Ovary — young seed sac at the base of a flower, usually hairy or scaly, becoming the seed capsule, which then dries and splits to shed seed by wind.

Umbel — the structure of the flower cluster, usually on a short stem or rachis, making it a racemose-umbel, capable of displaying up to 30 individual flowers.

LEAF AND SHOOTS

Bracts — protective sheath of leaflets that cover the emerging growth buds often highly coloured and attractive in the spring as they fall away from the new leaves.

Bullate — leaves with a puckered or raised surface between the veins.

Cuneate — the base of the leaf where it meets the petiole is wedge-shaped.

Decurrent — a ridge on the stem where the leaf stalk base meets, extending downwards.

Elliptic — a leaf that tapers evenly at both ends and is about twice as long as it is broad.

Glabrous — having no hairs on the leaf (or flower) parts.

Glandular — having hairs with glands at the tips that can leak sticky sap on leaves (or in flowers).

Indumentum — hairy or glandular covering of leaves, often woolly and long lasting underneath.

Mucronate — end of leaf, ending in a sharp point, the opposite being **emarginate** — a leaf ending in a small notch.

Lanceolate — narrow leaf, tapering to a point and 3–4 times longer than it is wide.

Obovate — slightly egg-shaped leaf with the narrow end at the petiole.

Oblanceolate — a combination of the above two, with a longer narrow egg-shape, broader at the tip.

Petiole — the leaf stalk.

Tomentum — hairy or glandular covering of stem, petiole and ovary, often woolly in appearance.

Bibliography

'La correspondance du Père Delavay a été analysée par Jean Lennon, Le Père Jean-Marie Delavay (1834-1895), un grand naturaliste français', *Bulletin de l'Association des Parcs botaniques de France*, vol. 38, 2004

Bailey, Lt-Col. F.M. *No Passport to Tibet*, Travel Book Club, USA, 1957

Bishop, George. *Travels in Imperial China*, Cassell, London, 1990

Briggs, Roy. *Chinese Wilson*, HSMO, Michigan, 1993

Coats, Alice. *The Quest for Plants*, Studio Vista, London, 1969

Cox, Kenneth (ed.). *F.K. Ward's Riddle of the Tsangpo Gorge*, Antique Collectors' Club, Suffolk, 2001

Cox, Peter & Cox, Kenneth. *The Encyclopedia of Rhododendron Species*, Glendoick Publishing, Perth, 1997

Cox, Peter & Hutchison, Peter. *Seeds of Adventure*, Garden Art Press, Suffolk, 2008

Cox, Peter. *The Larger Species of Rhododendron*, Batsford, New York, 1979

Davidian, H.H. *The Rhododendron Species*, Timber Press, Portland, 1989

Franchet, Adrien. 'Hommage au R.P. Delavay', *Journal de Botanique*, vol. 1er janvier 1896

Franchet, Adrien. 'Notice sur les travaux du R.P. Delavay', *Bulletin dit Muséum d'hist. natur.*, no. 4, pp. 148–151, 1896

Kilpatrick, Jane. *Fathers of Botany*, Kew Books, Surrey, 2014

Kingdon Ward, F. *Burma's Icy Mountains*, Jonathan Cape, London, 1949

Kingdon Ward, F. *From China to Hkamti Long*, E. Arnold, London, 1924

Kingdon Ward, F. *In Farthest Burma*, Seeley, Service & Co., London, 1921

Kingdon Ward, F. *Plant Hunter in Manipur*, Jonathan Cape, London, 1952

Kingdon Ward, F. *Return to the Irrawaddy*, A. Melrose, London, 1956

Kingdon Ward, F. *Rhododendrons for Everyone*, Gardeners' Chronicle, University of California, 1926

Kingdon Ward, F. *Rhododendrons*, Latimer House, 1949

Kneller, Mariana. *The Book of Rhododendrons*, David & Charles, Devon, 1995

Lancaster, Roy. *Travels in China — A Plantsman's Paradise*, Antique Collectors' Club, Suffolk, 1989

Mao, A.A., Bhaumik, M., Paul, A., Bharali, S. & Khan, M.L. '*Rhododendron mechukae* — A New Species from India', *Edinburgh Journal of Botany*, Vol. 70, Issue 01, pp 57–60, March 2013

McLean, Brenda. *A Pioneering Plantsman: A.K. Bulley and the Great Plant Hunters*, Stationery Office Books, London, 1997

McLean, Brenda. *George Forrest Plant Hunter*, Antique Collectors' Club, Suffolk, 2004

McLelland, John (ed.). *William Griffith — Journals of Travels in Assam, Burma, Bootan, Afghanistan and the Neighbouring Countries*, Munshiram Manoharlal Publishers, New Delhi, reprinted 2001

McQuire, J.F.J. & Robinson, M.L.A. *Pocket Guide to Rhododendron Species*, Kew Publishing, Surrey, 2009

O'Brien, Seamus. *In the Footsteps of Augustine Henry*, Garden Art Press, Suffolk, 2011

Pim, Sheila. *The Wood and the Trees, a biography of Augustine Henry*, MacDonald, 1966

Pradhan, Rebecca & Fellings, Wouter Jan. *Wild Rhododendrons of Bhutan*, Pradhan, Thimphu, Bhutan, 1999

Salley, H. & Greer, H. *Rhododendron Hybrids*, Batsford, New York, 1986

Singh, K.K., Rai, L.K. & Gurung, B. 'Conservation of *Rhododendrons* in Sikkim Himalaya', G.B. Plant Institute of Himalayan Environment and Development, *World Journal of Agricultural Sciences*, 5 (3): 284–296, IDOSI Publications, 2009

The London Gazette, 29 June 1897, re Robert Blair McCabe

Tiwari, Onkar N. & Chauhan, U. K. '*Rhododendron* conservation in Sikkim Himalaya', Department of Biotechnology, Ministry of Science and Technology, Lodi Road, New Delhi in *Current Science*, Vol. 90, No. 4, 25 February 2006

Turner, Samuel. *Account of an Embassy to the Court of the Teshoo Lama in Tibet; containing a narrative of a journey through Bootan, and part of Tibet in 1783*, A. & W. Nicol, 1749–1802

Tyler-Whittle, Michael. *The Plant Hunters*, Heinemann, Portsmouth, 1970

Opposite: *R. protistum* 'Pukeiti' (left), *R. rex* ssp. *rex* 'Quartz' (middle), *R. magnificum* (right).

Photographic credits

All photographs by Pat Greenfield except the following:

Abbotsbury Subtropical Gardens p. 127

Andrew Brooker pp. 90, 139,

Ashiho Mao pp. 64 (right), 71 (top), 72

Bodnant Garden p. 123

Crown Estate, Windsor p. 124

Glyn Church pp. 16, 18, 22 (bottom), 23 (both), 41 (top), 79 (right), 166, 168, 170

Graham Smith pp. 17, 26, 28, 29, 30, 32, 34 (left), 51 (top), 52 (bottom), 53, 54, 56 (top), 59 (bottom), 60, 63 (both), 65, 66 (bottom), 67 (top), 68 (both), 69 (left), 70 (both), 78 (top & middle), 80 (bottom, left), 84, 91, 92, 93 (bottom), 96, 104 (both), 105 (middle), 106 (top), 107 (all), 110, 111, 112, 115, 116, 119, 120 (both), 121, 122, 125, 130 (top), 131, 164, 169, 172, 173

Keith Rushforth pp. 45, 61 (top)

Ken Cox pp. 40 (right) 71 (bottom) 98, 99

Kew Gardens pp. 34 (middle), 35 (middle), 37, 39, 40 (left) 41 (bottom) 42 (top)

Lynn Bublitz p. 46

Mark Joel p. 57

Ray Cox Photography p. 47

Royal Botanic Garden Edinburgh p. 37

Steve Hootman pp. 19, 20, 22 (top), 24, 25 (both), 49, 50, 51 (bottom), 52 (top), 56 (right), 62, 66 (top), 69 (right) 87 (left, top), 89, 93 (top), 171

Tom Hudson pp. 44, 61 (bottom), 64 (left)

R. sinogrande.

With thanks…

This book has been a joy to create. All three of us have enjoyed the journey, and the camaraderie of crafting a book together. As ever there are heroes in the background who made it possible.

A very special thank you to five people who helped us so much with information about plants in the wild and for generously sharing their photographs:

> Steve Hootman, Rhododendron Species Foundation in Washington
>
> Keith Rushforth in Devon, England
>
> Tom Hudson in Cornwall, England
>
> Ken Cox in Glendoick, Perth, Scotland
>
> Dr Ashiho Asosii Mao in Shillong, India

For information and support — Michael Hudson, Sir Richard Storey, Lady Anne Berry, Keshab Pradhan, Alan Jellyman, Lynn Bublitz, Gordon Bailey, Jeremy Thompson, Sashal Dayal, David Sayers.

Susan Worthington and the late Max Kempson for encouragement and support.

Tracey Borgfeldt and Paul Bateman of Bateman Publishing for their patience and expertise, Caroline List for a marvellous job of editing the book, and Shelley Watson of Sublime Design for the perfect layout.

Andrew Brooker, Manager of Pukeiti Rhododendron Trust and Diane Jordan, secretary of the Trust for helping us at every turn.

The Pukeiti Rhododendron Trust and its members for their long-term support and financial backing, and the staff at Pukeiti for access to sixty years of records and information.

Derek Hughes for photographic assistance; and also Lynn Parker at Kew Gardens.

Librarian Pam Robinson for searching out lost tomes.

For translations: Latin — Beth Hill; French — Marilyn Herbert; Danish — Antona Wagstaff.

Taranaki Regional Council staff for their recent management of the Pukeiti collection.

Taranaki Savings Bank Community Trust for their financial backing.

Index

Page numbers in **bold** denote images.

Abbey, Captain 93
Abbotsbury Subtropical Gardens 126–7, **127**
Aberconway, Lord (McLaren) 106, 124
Abies 16, **16**, 17, **45**, 90, **139**, **166**, 167
Abinger, Lord (Captain James Scarlett) 121
Achamore Gardens 121, **121**
Alnus nepalensis 166–7
America, gardens in 31, 114–6
American Rhododendron Society 86, 173
'Annapolis Royal' hybrid 103
Ardkinglas Woodland Garden 119, **119**
Arduaine Garden **26**, **30**, 121–2
Arnold Arboretum 40–1
Arunachal Pradesh 18, 21, 22, 64, 71, 73, 168; species 46, 47, 50, 54, 59, 61, 63, 64, 71, 73, 77, 78, 84, 95, 168
Assam 23, 43, 128, 168; species 63, 77, 94, 95
Aster delavayi 37
Australia **52**, 106, 108, 129–30, **130**; growing conditions 31, 49, 113; species 122, 126, 159, 161, 166
Australian Rhododendron Society 129, 173
Awards of Garden Merit (AGM) 56, 66, 82
Awards of Merit 51, 52, 56, 63, 66, 67, 82, 87, 93, 95; foliage 50, 59, 66, 84; hybrids 103, 104, 105, 106, 108, 109, 110, 111
azaleas 37, **158**, 159

Balfour, Professor Isaac Bayley 42, 50, 51, 118; and George Forrest 37, 38, 50
'Barbara Hayes' hybrid **100**, 103, **103**
Barlup, Jim 110
Barsey Rhododendron Sanctuary, Sikkim **56**, 171
Bartram, John 15, 28
Basford, John 101, 117
beeches, National Collection 120

Beekman, J. 108
Bees Ltd, Bees Nursery 30, 37, 42
Benmore, Scotland **50**, **60**, **68**, 118; Benmore F.C.C. **85**, **86**; 'Benmore' KW 6261A 86
Berg, Warren 60
Betula utilis 167
Bhutan 16, 18, **18**, **22**, **23**, 158, 160, **166**; collectors in 35–6, 43, 45; overview 23–4, 168; Royal family 10, 79; species 45, 46, 53, 54, 58–9, 62, 63, **63**, 77, 78, 79, **79**, 118
Birk, Jens 111
bluebells **161**, 163
Bodnant Garden, Wales **123**, 123–4
Bolitho, Sir Edward 128
Bond, John 126
Booth, Thomas 16, 59
Borde Hill Gardens 108
Boscawen, John (J.T.) 102, 108
Boyle, Richard (Earl of Burlington) 28
Bridgeman, Charles 28
British gardens overview 28–31
Brodick Castle Garden **80**, 86, 101, **116**, 116–7; awards, certificates 50, 84, 90, 93, 105; 'Brodick' clones 50, 86; hybrids 105, 109
Broker, Geoff *see also* 'Geoff Broker' 105
Brooker, Andrew **46**, **144**
Brydon, P.H. (Jock) 115
Bulley, Arthur 30, 37, 42
Burlington, Earl of (Richard Boyle) 28
Burma 22, 35, 43, 47, 128; species 46, 50, 51, 65, 66, 82, 84, 89, 91, 93, **93**, 95
Burton Smith, Peta, Vinh 61

Caerhays Castle 30, 125, 127–8
Calcutta Botanic Garden 16, 55
Calcutta Journal of Natural History 77
Callander, James Henry 119
Campbell, Dr Archibald 34, 120
Campbell, Bruce 103
Campbell, Sir George 119
Campbell, Lady Grace 119–20

Campbell, Sir Ilay 120
Campbell family Arduaine Garden 122
Campbell family Stonefield Castle 120
Canada, gardens in 114
Cardiocrinum giganteum 5, 163, **163**
Carlyon, A.S.G; Major George Gwavas 131
Catesby, Mark 15, 28
Chamberlain, David 61, 118
'Charles' hybrid 103
'Cherry Tip' hybrid 66
China 18, 19–21, 27, **41**, 169; species 39, 67, 70, 94, 95, 98
China *see also* Yunnan, Sechuan
Church, Gail 22
Church, Glyn 22, **162**
Church Garden, New Zealand **156**
'Churchill' hybrid 103
Clark, Alan 21, 73, 96, 123, 127
Clarke, Colonel S.R. 108
Clyne Castle 104, 106; hybrids 104
Viscount Cobham (Sir Richard Temple) 28
'Coconut Ice' hybrid 110
'Colonel Rogers' hybrid 103–4, **104**, 108
companion plants 154–63, **156**, **157**, **158**, **159**, **160**, **161**, **162**, **163**
conservation 17–8, 165–7, 166–7, 169
Cook, Douglas 130
Cornus florida 156, **156**
Corsewell, Scotland 84
Cory, Reginald 37
Cox, Euan 47
Cox, Kenneth (Ken) 22, 47, **47**, 84; species collected 46, 59, 61, 63, 71, **71**, 73, 84, 85, 92, 131
Cox, Peter 47, **47**, 53, 59, 60, 70, 73, 131
Crarae Garden **53**, **54**, **56**, 104, 119–20, **120**; 'Crarae' hybrid 104
Cryptomeria japonica 158, **158**
cultivation *see* rhododendron growing
cuttings, propagation by 147–9, **148**

Darjeeling 33–4, 62
David C. Lam Asian Garden 20, 114

Davidia (handkerchief tree) 18, 40
Davidia involucrata (Dove Tree) **26**
Davidian, H.H. 118
Davidson, John 114
de Rothschild, Edmund 101, 103, 125–6; 'Edmund de Rothschild' 126
de Rothschild, Lionel 56, 101, 103, 104, 109, 126; *R. rothschildii* 68
Delavay, Jean Marie 19, 30, 36–7, 50, 66
Digby, Lord 111
diseases and pests 142-3
Douglas, David 119
Downie, John 109
Dulong Valley, Yunnan **19**, 89, 94
Duncan, James 118

Eastwoodhill Arboretum 130
Edinburgh Botanic Garden *see* Royal Botanic Garden Edinburgh
'Edmund de Rothschild' hybrid 126
'Elaine Rowe' hybrid 105
'Elsae' hybrid 102, 104
Emu Valley Rhododendron Garden, Society 129–30, **130**
endangered species 20, 64, 130, 172
England, gardens in 124–8
Ericaceae 45, 161
Ernest Wilson Collection **60**
Ethel Joel Garden, Dunedin **57**
'Evening' hybrid 106, 109
Exbury Gardens 56, 68, 103, 104, **125**, 125–6; awards 87, 104; *R. praestans* Exbury form **87**
'Eyestopper' hybrid 105

Fagaceae species 21, 96
Falconer, Hugh 55
Falconera subsection 16, 49, 117, 120, 126, 150
'Faltho' hybrid 111
Fang, W. P. 99
Farrer, Reginald 18, 47, 51, 93, 119, 124
Ferny Creek Horticultural Society 129
First Class Certificates 56, 77, 82, 84, 86, 90, 95; foliage 67; hybrids 104
Flora of British India 35
Forde, Patrick 61
Forrest, George 19, 27, 29, 36, **37**, 37–8; contributions 30, 117, 118, 124, 126, 127–8, 131, 135; species collected 50, 51, 52, 65, 67, 69, 71, 87, 89, 91, 93, 94, 166
Fortune, Robert 30
'Fortune' hybrid 56, 103, 104, **104**, 107, 126
Foster, Maurice 43
Franchet, Adrien René 36, 66

Ganderton, Nellie (Wilson) 40
Gaoligongshan National Nature Reserve 19, 51, 89, 94, 169
'Geoff Broker' hybrid 105, **105**, **154**
Gibson brothers 110, 118
Gigha hybrids 117
Gill of Falmouth 56
'Glen Rosa' hybrid 93
Glenarn, Scotland 55, 110, 117–8
Glendoick Gardens 47, **63**, 68, **69**, 108, 111
Glenkinglas, Lady Anne 119
'Glenshant' hybrid 105
'Golden Dawn' hybrid 105, **105**
Goodwin, Jack 130
Gordon, Mrs Dale 108
Gordon, Ron 103
'Gordon Collier' hybrid 102, 105, **105**
grafting, propagation by **144**, 149–51, 149–151, **150**, **151**
'Grand Prix' hybrid 106
'Grandex' hybrid 106
Grandia series 16, 75–7, 117, 120, 126, 150
Grant, Lachie 110
Grieg, Mary 115
Griffith, William 15–6, 22, 23, **35**, 35–6, 62, 77
Grimshaw, John 44
Guan, Professor Kaiyun 20
Gunnera chilensis **162**
Gwavas Garden 43, **59**, 131, **131**, **159**, **160**

Hackfalls Arboretum. New Zealand **156**
Haines-Watson, W.C. 98
Hair, Rob *see also* 'Ina Hair' 106
Hance, Dr Henry 36
'Harp Wood' *R. hodgsonii* 63
Harrer, Heinrich 86
'Hawk' grex 126
Hayes, Des 103
'Haze' hybrid 106, 109
Heneage-Vivian *see* Walker-Heneage-Vivian
Henry, Augustine 18, 21, 38–9, **39**, 70
Hilliers Manual of Trees and Shrubs 131, 138
'Himalayan Child' hybrid 106
Himalayan rhododendrons 15–6
Hodgson, Brian 33, 62
Hollard, Bernard 101, 108, 111
Hollard Gardens 111
Hooker, Sir Joseph 16, 33–5, **34**, 39, 117; species collected 55, 62, 77, *77*, 120
Hooker, Sir William 120
Hootman, Steve 22, 23, 45–6, **46**, 115, 168; species collected 54, 59, 61, 63, 69, 70, 71, 73, 82, 84, 94
Horlick family, Sir James 104, 121
hostas 161, **161**
Hudson, Carola 131
Hudson, Michael 43, 131
Hudson, Tom 21, 22, 43–4, **44**, 127, 131; species collected 61, 69, 70, 71, 94, 96
Hutchison, Peter 53, 59, 60
Huthnance, George 105, 106
hybrids, overview 101–2
hydrangeas 28, **152**, 154, 155, 160

Ilchester, Countess of 126
'Ina Hair' hybrid 106, **106**
International Dendrology Society 44, 79, 172
Inverewe Gardens 122, **122**

Jack, William 15
'Jack Anderson' hybrid **101**, 107, **107**
'James Deans' hybrid 107
Jane Goodall Institute 172
'Jean Church' hybrid 105
Jiaozishan, Yunnan **139**, 169, **169**
'Joy Bells' hybrid 107, **107**
Joyce, Joseph 107

'Joyce' hybrid   107
Jury, Felix   101
Jury, Les   101, 107
Jury Garden   **157**

Kent, William   28
Kesang Dorjii Wangchuck   79
Kew garden   35, 39
Khangchendzonga National Park   171
'Kildonan' clone KW9200 (*R. magnificum*)   84
Kingdon Ward, Francis (Frank)   18, 20, 22, 23, 29, **42**, 61, 140; biography   42–3; contributions   118, 123, 124, 126, 128, 131; species collected   46, 50, 51, 66, 67, 82, 84, 86, 89, 106
'Koenig Carola' hybrid   107, **107**
Kunming Botanic Garden   20
Kunming Institute of Botany   19, 20
Kyonganosla Alpine Sanctuary   172

Lamellen Garden, Cornwall   124
Lang, David   61
Langsang National Park   171
Laojunshan, Yunnan   39, 70, **70**, 169
'Laramie' hybrid   110
Larson, Hjalmar L.   101, 109
Lauraceae species   21, 96
layering, propagation by   149
Leach, David   101
'Leo' hybrid   126
Leonardslee Garden   106
'Les Boisen' hybrid   105
'Les Jury' hybrid   107
Lindera obtusiloba   **160**
Little, Micky   121
'Little Jessica' hybrid   108
Lobb, Thomas   15
'Loch Awe' hybrid   108
Loder, Sir Edmund   101, 109, 111
Loder, Sir Giles   101, 106, 109
'Loderi King George' hybrids   109
Ludlow (Frank) and Sherriff (George)   92, 118, 123

Mackenzie, Mairi   122
Mackenzie, Osgood   122
Macklin, Jean   **42**, 43

magnolias   28, 34, 37, 156, **156**, **157**, 158
Magor, Edward, Eric   124–5
Maire, Edouard-Ernest   67
Makalu Barun National Park   171
Malone, Bob   130
Mangles, J.H.   109
Manipur   18, 23, 82, 91, 168
'Mansellii' hybrid   109
McCabe, Robert Blair   82
McLaren, Charles and Laura (Lord Aberconway)   124
'Mecca' hybrid   108
Meconopsis betonicifolia   37
Meerkerk, Ann   111, 115–6
Meerkerk, Max   115
Meerkerk Rhododendron Gardens   **67**, **78**, 111, 115–6, **115**, **172**
'Michael Beekman' hybrid   108
'Middlemarch' hybrid   108
'Milton Hollard' hybrid   108, 111
Minterne House and Gardens   51, 111
'Mist' hybrid   106, 109
Monbeig, Abbé   52
Montrose, Duke of   116
Montrose, Mary (Molly) Duchess of   86, 116
'Mrs George Huthnance' hybrid   105
'Mrs Henry Agnew' hybrid   109
'Mrs J.P. Lade' hybrid   150
mulching   136–7
Muncaster Castle, Lord   123
'Muriel' hybrid   56, 106, 109
'My Delight' hybrid   109
Myanmar   21, **22**, 51, **165**
Myanmar *see also* Burma

Nagaland   18, 23, 45, 45–6, 82, **164**, 168
'Naomi' grex   126
National Collection beeches   120
National Pinetum   118
National Rhododendron Gardens, Australia   129
National Trust (England)   128
National Trust for Scotland   116, 120, 122
The Nature Conservancy, USA   172
Naxi language   19, 42
Needham, Edward   43, 127

Nepal   16, 25, **25**, 167, **170**, 170–1; species   54, 55, 63, 77, 158, 167
'New Plymouth City' hybrid   107
New Trees   44
New Zealand gardens   31, 130–2
New Zealand Rhododendron Association   110, 173
Noble, Sir Andrew, Michael   119
Nothofagus (beeches)   120
Nuttall, Thomas   59

Olinda State Forest, Australia   **52**, **106**, 129
O'Rourke, Hilary   130
Orridge, Caroline   39
'Our Kate' hybrid   109

'Pacific Rim' hybrid   109
Patrick, Piers   118
paulownia   155, **155**
'Percy Wiseman' hybrid   108
perennials, ground cover plants   161–3
pests and diseases   142–3
Phytophthora   134, 142
Pieris formosa var. *forresti*   **159**
pines, *pinus*   58, 122, 156, 158, **170**, 171
'Pink Frills' hybrid   105
Pochin, Henry   124
'Poet's Lawn' *R. hodgsonii*   63
'Powder Snow' hybrid   110
Pradhan, Keshab C.   24, 172
Price, Sir Rose   128
propagation   145–51, **150**, **151**
pruning   141–2
Prunus x *yedoensis*   **158**
Puddle, Charles; Frederick; Marton   124
Pukeiti Rhododendron Trust   19, **46**, 106, 130–1, **130**, **144**, **158**, **161**, **173**; hybrids   105, 107; propagation   **144**, **148**, **151**; species   15, 33, 48, 55, 56, 58, 59, 67, 74, 76, 78, 79, 80, 81, 82, 83, 85, 86, 87, 88, 89, 90, 91, 92, 93, 94, 95, 96, 97, **102**, **163**

'Quartz' *R. rex* ssp. *rex*   42, **67**

R. arboreum   25, **25**, 77, 91, **120**, **170**; hybrids   46, 82

R. *arboreum* var. *album* 109
R. *argenteum* 34, 77
R. *arizelum* **6–7**, **20**, **29**, **48**, **49**, 49–50, **50**; 'Brodick' 50; found 42, 50, 69; hybrids 65, 68
R. *arizelum* var. *rubicosum* (Rubicosum Group) 50
R. *auriculatum* 122
R. *balangense* 99, **99**
R. *barbatum* 25
R. *basilicum* 51, **51**
R. *burmanicum* 82
R. *calophytum* 109
R. *campanulatum* 25
R. *cinnabarinum* 25
R. *coriaceum* 52, **52**, 65; 'Morocco' 52
R. *coryphaeum* 51, 87
R. *dalhousiae* 77
R. *decipiens* 53
R. *degronianum* ssp. *yakushimanum* 111
R. *degronianum* ssp. *yakushimanum* Exbury form 110
R. *delavayi* 37
R. *elliottii* 128
R. *excellens* 97
R. *eximium* 58
R. *falconeri* **13**, 34, **35**, **53**, **54**, 55, **112**, 120, **120**, 122; found 24–5, 25, 36, 171; hybrids 53, 56, 107, 111
R. *falconeri* ssp. *eximium* **29**, 46, **57**, **58**, 58–9, **59**, 106
R. *falconeri* ssp. *falconeri* **32**, 54–7, **55**, 56, **56**; hybrids 58, 102, 103, 104, 106, 107, 108, 109
R. *fictolacteum* see also R. *rex* ssp. *fictolacteum* 37, 65
R. *galactinum* 20, 41, 60, **60**, 111
R. *giganteum* 91, 122
R. *grande* 36, **74**, 75–7, **76**, 120; found 24, 24–5, 25, **25**, 171; hybrids 102, 103, 104, 105, 106, **106**, 107, 109; and R. *argenteum* 34, 77
R. *grande* affinity 73
R. *gratum* 51
R. *griersonianum* 107
R. *griffithianum* 24, 36
R. *griffithianum* L & S 2835 118
R. *heatheriae* 45, 47, 61, **61**

R. *heliolepos* var. *fumidum* **17**
R. *hodgsonii* 24, **33**, **34**, 62–3, **63**; found 24, 24–5, 25, 36, **62**, 171, **171**; hybrids 58, 103, 104, 106, 108, 109, 110; and R. *decipiens* 53
R. *kesangiae* **18**, **23**, 45, **78**, 78–9, **79**, **168**; found 24, 36, 45, 46, 79, **79**; hybrids 53, 58, **63**
R. *kesangiae* KR 1737 127
R. *kesangiae* var. *album* 79
R. *lacteum* 108
R. *lanigerum* 85–6
R. *longesquamatum* 99
R. *macabeanum* **43**, **80**, 80–82, **81**, **82**, 128, **147**; found 43, 45, 82, **164**; hybrids 11, **13**, 46, 82, 105–111
R. *magnificum* **14**, **83**, 83–4, **84**, **174**; found 42, 43, 46; hybrids 101, 105, 107; 'Kildonan' clone KW9200 84
R. *magnificum* aff 73
R. *malayanum* 15
R. *mallotum* 71
R. *mechukae* 22, 64, **64**
R. *megaphyllum* 51
R. *mollianum* 86
R. *mollyanum* 86, 116
R. *montroseanum* 43, **43**, 85–6, 116; Benmore F.C.C. **85**, 86; 'Benmore' KW 6261A 86; as R. *sinogrande* 85
R. *niveum* 103, 104, 108, 111
R. *nuttallii* 97
R. *ponticum* 107, 149–50
R. *praestans* 51, 68, 69, 87, **87**; Exbury form 87
R. *preptum* 65
R. *protistum* 19, 20, **89**, **90**, **91**, 122, **137**, **165**; hybrids 105; and R. *magnificum* 83–4
R. *protistum* Hillier form **88**
R. *protistum* 'Pukeiti' **5**, 89, **90**, 105, **132**, **173**, **174**, **184**
R. *protistum* var. *giganteum* 19, 88, 89, 90, 166
R. *protistum* var. *protistum* 88–9, 90, 90–1
R. *pudorosum* 92
R. *regale* 51
R. *rex*. R. *galactinum* 52
R. *rex* 'Quartz' 42

R. *rex* ssp. *fictolacteum* 52, 66, 67, **172**; found 19, **65**, 66
R. *rex* ssp. *rex* **17**, 20, 67, **67**, **139**, **169**; hybrids 111; KW 4509 67; 'Quartz' **67**, **174**
R. *rothschildii* 42, 51, 68, **68**, 87
R. *semnoides* 51, 69, **69**, 87
R. *sidereum* **92**, 93, **93**; 'Glen Rosa' 93
R. *sinofalconeri* 20, 21, 39, 45, 70, **70**
R. *sinogrande* **15**, **33**, **94**, 94–5, **95**, **116**, 122, **176–177**; delavayi 37; found 19, 20, **21**, **22**, 73; hybrids 56, 85–6, 103, 104, 106, 107, 108, 110, 126
R. *sinogrande* var. *boreale* 95
R. *species nova* 73, 99; HECC#10010 73
R. *suoilenhense* 21, **44**, 45, **96**, 96–7, **97**; AC431 127
R. *taggianum* 128
R. *taliense* 19
R. *thomsonii* 25, 34, 111
R. *titapuriense* 22, 71, **71**, **72**
R. *wardii* 111
R. *watsonii* 20, 40, **40**, 41, 98, **98**, 99
R. *wattii* 46, 82
R. *wightii* 53
R. x *decipiens* 53
R. *yakushimanum* 110, 111
Ramsden, Sir John 123
'Rare' 172
Return to the Irrawaddy 50
Reuthe Nursery 104, 108
Rhododendron, Camellia and Magnolia Group, Royal Horticultural Society 126, 173
rhododendron growing 27–31, 137–43, 153–4; see also companion plants; pests; propagation; soil
Rhododendron Society of Canada 173
Rhododendron Species Botanical Garden 45–6, 114–5, 115, 173; *species nova* HECC#10010 73
Rhododendron Species Foundation, Seattle 19, 23, 60
rhododendron wood 166–7, 170–1
Rhododendrons for Everyone 140
The Rhododendrons of Sikkim 24, **34**, **35**
Rock, Joseph 19, **41**, 41–2, 124; species collected 50, 51, 66, 68

Rogers, Colonel   103; 'Colonel Rogers' 103–4, **104**, 108
'Ronald' hybrid   110
Roots and Shoots   172
Royal Botanic Garden, Edinburgh   19, 37, 42, 59, 60, 118
Royal Gardens, Windsor   106
Royal Horticultural Society   117. *see also* Awards; Veitch Memorial Medal
Royal Horticultural Society Rhododendron Group   73, 126
Royal Society   35
Royston Nursery   115
Rubicosum Group   50
Rushforth, Heather   61
Rushforth, Keith   21, 22, 44–5, **45**, 127; species collected   51, 61, 73, 96
Rutherford Conservatory   115

Sagarmatha National Park   171
Saharanpur Gardens   55
Sargent, Charles Sprague   40–1
Savill, Sir Eric   124–5
Savill Garden (Windsor Great Park) **124**, 124–5
Scarlett, Captain James   121
scions   **150**, **151**
Scotland, gardens in   116–22
Seattle Rhododendron Society *see also* Rhododendron Species Foundation   116
seedlings   **151**
seeds, propagation from   145–7
sequoiadendrons   118
Serbithang (plant collection)   24
Shamrock Hydrangea Collection, France   155
Sherriff, George   92, 118, 123
Shey Phoksundo National Park   171
Shingba Rhododendron Sanctuary, Sikkim   171
shrubs as companion plants   159–61
Sichuan   19, 20, 21, 40; species   60, 67, 98, 99
Sikkim   18, **24**, 24–5, 33–4, **62**, **171**, 171–2; species   **25**, 53, 54, 55, **56**, 63, 77, 103, 120

Sikkim Adventure Botanical Tours and Treks   24
Smith, Graham   101, 105, 107, 130
soil and drainage   16, 133–6
Soulié, Abbé   52
South Lodge, UK   77, 95
'Spiced Honey' hybrid   107, 110, **110**
Stevenson, J.B.   125
Stonefield Castle   **29**, **32**, 77, **112**, 120, **120**
Stowe garden   28
Strone Woodland Garden   119
Sullivan, Noel   130
'Surprise'; 'Surprise Packet' hybrid   111
Swan, George   150
Sykes, Colonel   55

Tagg, Harry   60
Taliensia subsection, *taliensis*   19, 99
Taranaki Regional Council   131
Temple, Sir Richard (Viscount Cobham)   28
Thomson, Dr Thomas   34
Thornley family   118
'Thoron Hollard' hybrid   111, **111**
Thrumshingla National Park   168
Tibet (Xizang)   16, 20, 21, 43, 45; species   47, 50, 52, 61, 63, 66, 69, 71, 84, 86, 87, 92, 95
tourism   20–5, 31, 61, 167, 168, 169, 171, 172
trees as companion plants   154–8
Tregothnan gardens   102
Trengwainton Gardens   82, 128
Trevanion family   127
Trewithen, Cornwall   95
Tsuga, tsuga dumosa   16, 17, 21, 94, 96, 158, 167

University of British Columbia Botanical Garden   20, 114, 115
USA, gardens in   31, 114–6
Valley Garden (Windsor Great Park)   124–5
Veitch Memorial Medal   24
Veitch Nurseries   15, 18, 40, 124, 127
Vietnam   21, 39, 43, **44**, 45, 172; species   45, 70, **70**, 96–7, 127, 147

Vireya rhododendrons   15, 86, 115, 129, 130

Wales, gardens in   123
Walker, Dr Milton   115
Walker-Heneage-Vivian, Admiral Algernon   104, 106
Wallich, Nathaniel   16
Ward, Francis (Frank) Kingdon *see* Kingdon Ward
Waterer, J.   111
Watt, Sir George   82
Weyerhaeuser Company   114–5
Wharton, Peter   20, 114
'Whidbey Island' hybrid   111
'White Dane' hybrid   111
Wight, Robert   36, 77
Williams, John Charles (J.C.)   30, 37–8, 125, 127–8
Williams, Michael   127
Wilson, Ernest (E.H.)   18, 29, 30, 39, **40**, 40–1, 60, **60**, 98, 124, 127
Windsor Great Park (Savill Garden)   52, 63, 124–5
Wolong Panda Reserve   99
woodland gardens   28–31, **152**
World Heritage sites   19
World Wildlife Fund   172
Wright, Edmund, Harry   122
Wright Smith, William   118

Xizang (Tibet)   21

Younger, Harry   118
Younger Botanic Gardens, Scotland   86
Younghusband, Sir Francis   86
Yunnan   16, **19**, 19–20, **20**, **139**, 169, **169**; collectors in   36–9, 42, 43, 117; species   **17**, **49**, 50, **50**, 51, **52**, 65, **65**, 66, 66–71, **70**, 87, 89, **89**, 91, 93–5, 156

Page 184: *R. protistum* 'Pukeiti'.

The authors

GRAHAM SMITH is a renowned world expert on rhododendrons. A graduate of Kew Gardens Diploma course, he emigrated to New Zealand in 1968 where he was appointed as curator of the Pukeiti Rhododendron Trust in Taranaki, and then became the director for 40 years before retiring in 2009. During his time at the helm, Pukeiti went from a raw collection of mostly hybrid rhododendrons to become the most diverse collection of the species in the world. He has a knack for breeding rhododendrons and has named and registered many new varieties. He established the Register of New Zealand rhododendron hybrids in 1978 when on the council of the NZRA and affiliated this to the International Register. He has gained a reputation as a popular speaker in the USA and in Britain as well as at rhododendron conferences around the world and he is a popular leader on botanical tours to China, Europe and Britain. Graham was made an Associate of Honour of the Royal New Zealand Institute of Horticulture, (AHRIH) in 2007. He brings a wealth of knowledge and experience, combining refined botanical detail with practical, down-to-earth information.

Now retired, Graham still maintains involvement with Pukeiti through the Taranaki Regional Council ownership, working with officers and staff on future planning and development as a community asset.

GLYN CHURCH has spent a lifetime growing and studying plants. Three years study at Pershore College of Horticulture in Worcestershire, then a spell of gardening for the rich and famous in London was followed by three years at the Chelsea Physic Garden where he gained his true plant knowledge. He then studied with the Royal Horticulture Society and gained a masters degree in horticulture.

In 1977 he and his wife Gail emigrated to New Zealand and for the last 25 years they have run a small nursery specialising in rhododendrons and more recently in hydrangeas, as well as turning ten acres of paddock into a botanical collection and garden. Glyn has also found time to write and publish six books, five of which were also published in England and America. All of these books were in collaboration with photographer Pat Greenfield.

Glyn and Gail are life members of the International Dendrology Society and have travelled extensively with them to study forests around the world, including the Appalachians, Florida, California, Korea, China and Bhutan.

PAT GREENFIELD was educated in England and New Zealand and travelled widely as a child, developing a strong interest in painting and writing, which eventually drew her to photography. When she moved to Taranaki she was able to combine her love of writing and photography, and her articles and photographs have subsequently featured in many magazines.

Pat researched, photographed and wrote about Pukeiti in tandem with Graham Smith, which culminated in a book on the gardens in 1997. She also teamed up with Glyn Church to produce a further six books on plants utilising her exquisite photographs. One of the books was on New Zealand plants, the other five books were more universal in content and released in the USA and the UK. As a measure of their artistic quality, the books are for sale in the Uffuzi gallery in Florence, Italy.

Pat has recently completed a ten year study of the rapidly eroding Taranaki coastline in conjunction with the regional Puke Ariki Museum. This geological and photographic study resulted in an exhibition at Puke Ariki in 2004. Pat also featured in a long-running exhibition called 'Blood, Earth, Fire' at the New Zealand national museum, Te Papa in Wellington.